NOMADIC JOURNEY

SPIRITUAL AWAKENING, SEEKING WISDOM, AND DISCOVERING GOD'S PLAN BY ACKNOWLEDGING OUR GIFTS AND TALENTS

LEE C. SMITH

BALBOA.
PRESS

A DIVISION OF HAY HOUSE

Scripture quotations marked KJV are from the Holy Bible, King James Version (Authorized Version). First published in 1611. Quoted from the KJV Classic Reference Bible, Copyright © 1983 by The Zondervan Corporation.

Balboa Press books may be ordered through booksellers or by contacting:

Balboa Press
A Division of Hay House
1663 Liberty Drive
Bloomington, IN 47403
www.balboapress.com
1 (877) 407-4847

Print information available on the last page.

ISBN: 978-1-9822-1580-4 (sc)
ISBN: 978-1-9822-1582-8 (hc)
ISBN: 978-1-9822-1581-1 (e)

Library of Congress Control Number: 2018913302

Balboa Press rev. date: 11/06/2018

CONTENTS

PROLOGUE: THE LIFE OF A JOURNEYMAN

Early Beginnings

It is simple really, the life _he_ (substitute **I** _he_re) was born into…

You don't just become such a man. His destiny was already chosen, he just had to step into it.

Life's experiences just strengthen one's resolve and shape the personality. Because his path was set by nature, the journeyman becomes a collector of many things…some unexplainable.

This nomadic life is not for all to understand or even live in—though the many spectators are curious and would want a glimpse into my introverted life—the thing of it all is, would they understand and truly accept me for who I am? The truth of the matter is that "Only a select few daring souls who have stepped off the path would truly understand; the rest just following previous trail marks would understand safety in what has already been done."

This solitary life is not all bad. There are moments of "planting" (self-awareness), but eventually some inner voice, "whisper," takes off and the movement begins.

Early Readings: Philosophy & Psychology—My early discovery of feeling the Universal Creator's (God's) Call But Not Understanding What It Meant to be Called

"The end to aim at is assimilation to God"
Plato (427-347 B.C.) in Diogenes Laertius

As a young teen, I found that I was an introvert, having very few true friends but able to blend into the circles of all the groups around me. For instance, I grew up in a military community near a local North Carolina beach. We had the islanders and the long-time civilians, the military folks and their retirees who were stationed or lived on the military bases or nearby in the local communities, and all this was good for the small businesses in the area.

I spent a great amount of time participating in seasonal sports in the neighborhood like any teen boy but found that was as far as my social skills went. When it came to building childhood relationships and friends I was awkward.

Because we spent so much time in church and other religious activities friends were few, and that made visiting my mom's hometown where we went to church an event. Since my father was studying or being an intern of sorts in visiting churches, we would spend nearly all day and the early evenings in service. The only advantage to this was getting to be first at the lunch or dinner line. As children, my four siblings and I were paraded through all the church activities and it felt like a never-ending pilgrimage to biblical learning from long Sundays, mid-week Bible studies, and even summer Bible school. The crazy thing was, my parents never really sat with us or taught us about religion or taught us how to read the Bible as a family. We learned it from the countless hours sitting in the pews, dreaming of the breaks between church services. Growing up Baptist perhaps "wasn't all bad." I certainly didn't understand much of it—meaning the differences in the numerous Church signs we would pass towards our Missionary Baptist Church.

During the late 1970s and early 1980s, our television was limited to only a few channels by the rabbit ear antennas. Much of the time the picture was lost when the antenna fell off to one side or the other. During this time of limited television and fewer moments of parental guidance, the movie Excalibur piqued my interest. King Arthur, with the council of Merlin, became the wisest of kings, and Merlin himself would became the famed mystical advisor. Though only a fable, something about Merlin's ability as a prophet and a wizard intrigued me. So much so, I began looking outside the box of normal religion but never understanding why. The normal tradition for me would be to know the 10 Commandments, the Lord's Prayer, and Revelations as my most basic of ideals. Unfortunately, after having to attend so many church services and summer sessions, I withdrew inside only to ignore most of the teachings until later in life. During this time of rebellion, it occurred to me that being an active, participating Baptist was a chore, not a desire. I had to memorize several scriptures for children's time in front of the church, the time of the service when we all give thanks to God for our blessings by reciting a verse from the Bible and being blessed by the minister. Having one foot in the church and one out, the following verse said it best, "Ye are they which have continued with me in my temptations." Luke 22:28

Though the verse talks about life and how temptations are always upon us, we like Jesus have a choice to do everything we can to fight them. As humans, sometimes that doesn't always work out so well, but somewhere as we fumble through life we make some pretty good discoveries. Though I would spend most of my life floating between groups in school and eventually joining the military, I found that I had a curiosity for philosophy.

I don't know how it happened or what the initial spark was but all I can remember was something in a civics class or through some divine intervention of the Universal Creator, Plato, Socrates, and Da Vinci would suddenly influence me in my late teens and early twenties.

The Republic, written by the Greek philosopher Plato, was one of the world's most translated and influential books of all time and would be one of the most important books I would ever read. The reading was not normal English as we speak today but I understood it and could find peace in its words and meaning beyond anything I could even understand. Even today, looking back, I didn't realize it was a part of the psychology and philosophy mix I enjoy learning and sharing with others, and little did I know its metaphysics would have such an impact not only on me but on so many people in the world.

> *"Imagine you have been imprisoned all your life and in a dark cave. Your hands and feet shackled and your head restrained so that you can only look at the wall straight in front of you. Behind you is a blazing fire, and between you and the fire a walkway on which your captors carry statues and all sorts of objects. The shadows cast on the wall by these objects are the only things you and your fellow prisoners have ever seen, all you have ever thought and talked about." Allegory of the Cave, appears in Book 7 of the Republic*

While there is much debate about the reading, I believe the explanation is that the cave represents "the realm of becoming"—the idea that ordinary people in an imperfect world are constantly changing.

I would graduate high school and join the U.S. Army and immediately after training be sent to Germany. There I would find the next stage of my "changes": Germany would be the critical planting (development of my maturity and awareness to what culture and language meant, to individuals and societies). Seeing this firsthand as an expatriate, living life outside my birth country (*USA*), anything I ever knew growing up in a small town would now seem like an episode of some reality show.

What lays ahead in this book are ideas seen from years of travel, living abroad, and in some cases channeling (receiving messages, before I understood what channeling meant). I hope you enjoy the journey of CHANGE in yourself as you share my testimonies and stories of my unusual reality both real and imagined, because I have come to accept "NORMAL" was not in my future, like being a non-traditional student going to the University at the age of 27.

I continue to enjoy the evolutions and shifts I am making in my spiritual and energetic awakening; not only in my understanding, but also in how to communicate and feel the energy around us/me. The more I accept from the Universal Creator's essence of energy, the more abundance is given to me. I hope this book of stories, blog entries, poems, and messages inspire you to begin a Journey with me, into living on the ENERGY!!!

The Universe is sharing with us, leading us, providing for us, and mentoring us. All we should do is accept that we are not always in control. And when we are tested or sent through detested tribulations, the intent is to accept that there are Angels, people and spiritual entities that introduce themselves to us so that we may be alerted to mile markers of changes that assist our growth as Light workers (healers, teachers, coaches, and more). All the people we meet and the experiences we collect over our lifetime are there to offer us a foundation to receive our next stage of illumination.

I can share from my personal experience the first two spiritual and energetic shifts that transpired and the spark that went off in my head from that evolution. Of recent, my curiosity about and studies into metaphysical spirituality have led me to now understand that my CROWN CHAKRA WAS AWAKENING!!!

As I share my journey and the messages of others I have met along the way, my understanding of ALIGNMENT of the CHAKRA has increased. I am just early in my studies about Universal balance, and the use of TAROT, CHANNELING, MEDITATION, and more.

Come on! Let's partner in this new discovery of SELF and our emerging PARTNERSHIP with those that are recruited to see the BEST IN YOU. I caution you, as you begin to see not with your eyes but your SPIRIT, your surroundings will no longer be the same. Friends and associates may change, and so much more will happen. But don't shy away. This is the Creator's (God's) way

PREFACE

When the "Bee Dream" came to me, I was sitting on my "rack," in my case a bottom bunk in a corner of a concrete room with a few other people working with me, in an undisclosed location outside Amman, Jordan. My bunk is a corner bunk in a room of three other bunks. I sleep, eat, rest, and unwind behind the door. Walled off by water bottle boxes and two wall lockers so that you can't see me when you walk in, the room is made to look like a maze for some privacy. We all have makeshift curtains hanging off the top end of our bunks secured with parachute cord that we get by the yards (green cord for securing everything). When my curtain is open during the day, I can see out of one of the two windows, which is good now that I am on a bottom bunk. Seniority is the name of the game, meaning the guy who has been in the room the longest gets the bottom bunk and choice bedding.

After spending a couple months on the top bunk, the previous crew has rotated back to the U.S. I now have the sole space that does not have rotation bed accommodations. Therefore, I have my Army footlockers on the top bunk: a wall locker used solely for a pantry for food supplies and junk food that I get mailed from family and friends. My other locker is for clothes and toiletries.

In addition, in front of the empty stacked water boxes I have an orange-colored three-drawer plastic self so I can store random supplies. On top of my wall lockers is my Army issue field gear for cold and combat. On my makeshift nightstand, a box of water bottles lays next to my computer and headphones. We all have headphones with microphones so we can Skype home when we can and watch movies and TV shows with the Wi-Fi that is provided to us.

During my stay in Jordan, I had made several trips near the Syrian border, to the Jordan River, the Dead Sea, and other areas of religious or historical interest. My time in the country was government-related; however, I found time to see some of the country, interact with its people, and develop a deeper understanding of myself.

Since 2011, I have been on a soul journey, a mind shift, and a personal development crusade to become more sage-like, having the ability to be like Moses, Solomon, King David, Thales of Miletus (Know thyself), Pittacus of Mytilene (Know thy opportunity), Buddha, Gandhi, and others who have used their natural gifts to help others. Over the course of my life, I have known I have had the ability to counsel and inspire those that need it. As the years have passed, my appreciation for European, Asian, American Indian, Arabian, and so many other cultural traditions *showed me more about the basics of humanity we least take time to look at.* Developing countries like Kuwait, Iraq, Jordan, Qatar, and other places where my comrades-in-arms serve are reminders of how America started to formalize a culture or brand its society (America is known as "The Land of Opportunity"). Regions like Afghanistan, much of Africa, and other underdeveloped countries are reminders that people who come from the same background don't always see eye to eye or have the same vision for individual or societal views on how to live a FULFILLED life. Like those developing countries even the USA is slow to develop because of government or traditional family or religious rule. Any country that suppresses individuals and/or a society's development because of POWER or EGO are only hindering the potential of the whole, which affects the ENERGY not only of its people but its natural resources. For example, Global Warming, discrimination, poverty, and continual extinction of species are all byproducts of misuse and ignorance to the effect human NEGATIVE intervention causes to the World. Don't get me wrong! The United States has its social and political issues too, not just in socio-economic and geo-political scales but also in determining how natural and other limited resources are to be used and who gets them. In countries that are less developed, I've come to appreciate the privileges of:

❖ Sanitation pick up
❖ Clean drinking water (higher standards)
❖ Ability to travel without restrictions (out of country or between borders)
❖ Rights for equality (gender, economic, and race)

All cultures and all religions have been of interest to me, and during the last two deployments in as little as three years meditation and setting intentions have been my latest discoveries. From these new developments I was beginning to feel a draw to the Universe and its Creator. For some, that is God or some other Higher Power. I use both Universal Creator and God interchangeably depending on with whom I am speaking.

Most dreams *elude remembrance* but for the one I will share with you in the next pages I was compelled to document the message because the clarity of the dream in content and image were so strong that it gave my spirit or soul a mission I could not ignore. The dream was the planting of my "tree-soul." The ideas that would later be discovered were pollinated because several bees had delivered the much-needed pollen to assist in my spiritual and human growth.

What it meant to me may be something different for you. Nonetheless, it will be the "catalyst" for your awakening as it jolted my own higher spirit and awareness to the ENERGY in the world of manifesting and setting intentions; that the power of understanding would help align how I would begin to study the art of balancing my Chakra, an ancient philosophy to balance your body and mind using Eastern wellness beliefs, having seven centers that govern all your organs and work together independently yet as one system.

Using these new ideas of Eastern and Middle Eastern experiences, your circle of positive "light" people (supporting cast) will be your lifeline to the unexpected but energetic power, to the "God spark" that lies within you.

In the following pages, you will transform your vision and learn about what it means to be a Local, Regional, or Global Thinker. Over the years, I have noticed clusters and attitudes of many who remain, shift, or relate to a type of cluster (stay in groups that fit their comfort).

The Dream: Bees

The Messengers

A Soul's Journey: What the Bees Should Say!
**A Parable of Bees and a new look at your belief
system, your views of life, and how you think.**

To YOU The Reader:

When I write stories, poems, or artistic messages from somewhere
above my head, I am not always present to what is being told
until after the message is complete. Just like in my dreams, I don't
understand at the time what is going on, but somehow my soul
and intuition are translating the messages and letting me know
their importance.

Now it is time to share with you the dream:

The Dream...Bees

Confidence is a good thing, as well as determination and a desire to succeed in anything that you set your mind to. I can look back on my journey and look at my faults and those events (distractions) that had nothing to do with my personal growth. However, some random interruptions would prepare me for the current path I am on: purposefully seeking the Universal TRUTH in all things.

It is amusing dealing with people who embrace you on one hand for your natural or learned talents or competencies (especially in the workplace), while those same people (at leisure or public spaces) might say you are a dreamer, weird, maybe even conceited, arrogant, and more.

I think we all have different sides we show to people in our work, at home, in public, and at play. There is no denying that sometimes we boast about our abilities. We sometimes must believe we are not bad or unworthy of more when others don't believe in us. Our belief in ourselves is like a SHIELD (which can mean: Show How I Encourage and Lift my own Desires) when others don't think we deserve or are capable of accomplishing something. And when we succeed, many times those who would put us in our place take the credit for our accomplishments.

I have and continue to read a lot of books, listen to a lot of stories, and take a lot of negative criticism from a set of people who may very well be as lost as I am. No one wants to feel that their vulnerabilities are exposed or that they are weak or not important.

To those people, I say: I have fears too, but getting all we desire and want in the "package we desire" doesn't always translate into reality due to obligations, time, and resources.

Two books that come to mind have left me with lasting quotes I will always carry with me. They are written in the diary I keep, and are a reminder to the things I want to go back and read. Intentions, manifesting, coaching, teaching, learning, and just absorbing are things that are important in my search for fulfillment and understanding (Seeking the Spiritual Knowledge) that balances and enriches my life.

> "Poor people talk about cars and clothes, middle class people speak of education and jobs, but the rich speak of investments, wealth, and careers (that point you are doing what you love and earning without doing a thing; exceptions yes—wealth is not always defined in economic terms)."
> The Wealth Choice

> "God does not call the qualified, he qualifies the called."
> The Circle Maker

We are finally to the dream…Bees.

Things are going well in my life. Not perfect, not certain. But I have a feeling that there is no burden that I must carry now. I make my prayers of my desires that I need to keep praying for: "I AM desirable, I AM worthy, I AM what you made me oh GOD, I AM favored, and I AM more than they will see or understand."

Sin and Blessings are two sides of the coin when it comes to light and dark ENERGY. I believe there are evil (Fallen Angels or Wayward (unclean) Spirits) in the world; they test, tempt, and manipulate you and push you in ways that you question your consciousness. Do they even know they are doing it? Satan—oh let me tell you—the games—the attacks—hence the dream. I fall short of glory too—oh yes! I am a human being. I am taught, and I observe, and I know what right and wrong are but I still sin, choosing at times to do the wrong thing because it is easier than taking the time to do the right thing. For example, at a crosswalk there is a light that signals it is safe to cross; however, if traffic is light and I can cross safely I won't wait for that light.

In the dream, I am standing directly in front of a door—how crazy, right? Normally we try not to stand directly in front of a door so others can enter. In addition, I am apparently standing in another doorway, which is similar to the first, and I am watching myself. The room is white and plain, with no real furniture except a white board. I can see it is a beautiful sunny day, because the room in which I am watching myself goes directly to the outside. Unlike the door where I am standing, there is a room but nothing more than that. There is no furniture, no pictures, and no real sense I am standing on the floor or ground. I am not floating but I am in a room bare of "stuff." I realize later that there is another door to my right.

There are people here, but without recognizable faces or voices, and I am talking and smiling with them. Suddenly, a bee comes buzzing around me (#1 me). I am not frightened. However, I don't want this bee to bother me, so I swat it away nicely. But it becomes aggressive. "Oh you have to die now," I think to the bee. "I am sorry, but it is you or me." So, I swat him with a book. I can't explain where the book came from. Dreams are like that.

I resume laughing and talking with random people. Another bee arrives. "Oh, I am not having this." So I start talking all sorts of junk to this bee—"Oh you really want to battle with me? You're a small creature that I must take out. Don't you see what happened to your buddy on the floor over there? He is dead. Do you really want to go down like that? Keep messing with me... are you kidding?" The bee, however, is undeterred.

I am still watching myself (#2 me) from the other door. "It sure is bright outside," says I (#3 me). Yes, there is a third me in a third doorway. I glimpse my car. Like most dreams, it was a quick realization but no significance as to having known why it was noted or even what kind of car. But it is mine; somehow I just know it. From the door across the room, I am watching my other (#1) self talk trash to a bee. Really, what is that about, I ask the inside door me (#2)? (While I am splintered into three people we are all the same, existing at the same time.) At any rate, I am watching this and think, this is kind of amusing. I am cracking myself up.

Then I hear the bee talk. Did that bee just talk to the outside door me (#3)? Yes, it did. What? I do not understand. Outside, there is nothing but bright light and white walls that I can assume are buildings but there are no markings, except the lines where there are edges to this dream.

The outside door me (#3) says, "Oh bee, I hate to tell you but I am bigger, stronger, smarter, and the Alpha over you. You are going down." SWAT! The bee is down—now there are two dead bees that have hit the floor.

I can't believe this! The inside door me (#2) is witnessing a third bee. Are you kidding?! The outside door me (#3) is also looking like what the… (trying not to cuss).

But this bee is bigger and he is talking smooth, "I see you killed two of my friends and I can't let that go."

So outside door me (#3) is like, "I didn't start this but I feel I had the right to defend myself."

The third bee replies, "Really? Tell me how those two little bees scared you so much that you had to talk trash and then SWAT them."

Inside door me (#2) is like (thinks)…Oh my?! A smart bee. Let's see where this is going.

So the third bee is smiling but I see outside door me (#3) looking perplexed to the point of annoyance (by now you are wondering why #3 me has little patience and is quickly angered— he is not violent but he is acting out because he has never been in this situation before. Have you ever tried hiding your fear by acting out?). Bested by a bee? Come on!

Outside door me (#3) finally says, "Let me tell you something..." The rest is not coherent.

I can't hear my side of the conversation, but this came loudly and clearly from the bee, "You assaulted those two and hurt them because they annoyed your ears, buzzed around your head.... They had a message you didn't hear. Well, let me show you what a hoard of bees have to say!"

Suddenly inside door me (#2) runs right past the outside door me (#3) and we are now one (#'s 1-3).

I (now we) run outside to the right door near where the once inside-door me (#2) stood. We exit the door, hang a left, and round the corner to what looks like a big industrial area. But it is clean and white. My car is not too far in front of me, but I will never make it. I thought the bees were following, and they did for a split second, but I slammed the door to the room on my way out.

However, as I look at the car and begin in that direction the third bee is waiting. And he is signaling the hoard of bees to attack. I have a smoke grenade and a white board. I pop the grenade, throw it in front of me, and move the white board into the center of the smoke in front of me.

The bees are coming regardless of the smoke.

The smoke clears and the bees are stuck to the white board. They are done, except number three. He is stunned but he slowly buzzes over and tells me, "You have done something most have not and that is you thought through your actions before you acted. But you are not clear yet."

I am confused like no other now ("my brains are scrambled eggs"), but I look at this bee in a different light. I want to run to my car but there is no need. There are no people around us. Just me and the bee. It is so bright out.

Suddenly, I awake with a calm feeling but I feel there is something I should take from this.

BIG PAUSE

Well, even from the first day of waking I felt the dream meant keeping my wits about me and maintaining my tongue. I don't have to prove to anyone who I am, what I can do, or try to explain how I got what I have and what I don't.

But in the last few weeks I let Satan play mind games and I didn't trust my intuition or have faith in my life had purpose. Because of that self-doubt, I lost "Round One." This was a warning: Don't lose yourself in the masses of the hoard and let your PRIDE get the best of you. No one succeeds on their own. Change starts within you but support comes from those that bring Light around you.

PRIDE, FAITH, HOPE, CHANGE, and SUCCESS are all manifested in your beliefs—whether you're poor or rich your ability to cope in adversity can be sign of your vulnerability when things are out of control, when you are being tested. But you can be the TIP of the SWORD and steadfast in your faith and overcome harsh conditions. I have touted some past accomplishments but those are finished. I have to look forward to a new beginning, start a new journey. Where I am going and what I am doing today, my willingness to accept that I can fail but I can also accomplish great deeds sets me apart from my old beliefs and my family DNA of negative energy. Risk is one of the biggest variables between people staying AVERAGE or being ABOVE AVERAGE.

I will focus on my CHOICE to be ABOVE AVERAGE. Oh yes! Because I AM more than I can even imagine, and even more when I pray, meditate, and manifest good action. But I will continue to seek HIS (GOD, Universal Creator…) guidance and have faith that my direction is the right one FOR ME! Keep your PRIDE (ego) in check and follow your spirits' calling.

Ideas, Blog Entries, and Evolving Beliefs

The Philosopher

A Personal Journey: A Calling
Life Without Wisdom, Understanding, and Application is a Life Unrealized

God's Highway Project

Most citizens look for road improvements on interstates so that they can have smoother rides for long distance driving and to accommodate high speeds; however, cracks, potholes, and other debris still find the driver's car, leaving the scars of travel.

For those looking for help on county and city roads, the dangers and concerns are nearly the same as on the highway, except there are reduced speeds and safer roads because of housing in the area. But again, similar problems to those of the interstate still exist.

Those living in remote areas have little aid for road repair from the county in which they live, so they must rely on themselves to keep their dirt or gravel-filled roads usable. In addition, their concerns are not so much on safety as usability.

Regardless of one's needs our roads continue to need upkeep and maintenance. I have been fortunate to notice layers of improvements to roads (interstates, county, city, and private) at times. When you look closely enough, you sometimes see the making of roads or their decay; i.e., dirt, concrete, asphalt, and more are compositions of many highways. However, in some layers there are brick and other compounds to make a road drivable. Like the highway maintainers they try to use affordable and updated materials to take care of the road. This amount of science and care to maintain a safe road system is crucial.

God does the same for us too. The Bible is our instruction book or foundation for how to live. For many who believe in the Bible its stories are crucial. Every so often, He challenges us or puts trials in our way to improve our souls. Sometimes the process has major delays like that of a highway project. Have you ever seen road improvements in your town or someplace you travel and say, "It has been years and they still are not finished!" or "Is there always construction on this road?" I am sure you have. I recall saying such things about long, never-ending construction projects.

Watching a bridge or building project delay or something of high value being constructed over time suddenly abandoned or delayed has you pondering what could have caused a work stoppage. Like our hearts and souls, we too sometimes call out for conservancy only to have the call delayed or unheard, or so we think (Who can tell what or when the Universal Creator or God will answer?). Negotiations for highway projects sometimes interfere with the much-needed work at hand; approval to move forward in a project is either accepted or declined possibly because bids are bad, the town or county can't afford to help pay for improvements, or the state ties up funds in its budget.

Life is like that as well: Our souls and hearts need care and sometimes it does not come when we want it. Like projects that get started, sometimes roadblocks happen, with inferior materials being delivered, budget issues slowing things down, or sometimes it is simply nature not cooperating. Our lives are like that too; we are distracted, we procrastinate, we get depressed, or we are just overwhelmed. Just like construction projects, some days it seems like our soul's journey, just like a construction venture, is moving right on schedule and we feel the road and its traffic are moving in our favor, but then comes the dreaded accident or natural disaster or some other interruption to our travel plans or road plan (life-purpose interruptions due to illness, death, birth, changes…).

What do we do? We ask, "Why are there delays?" "Was I speeding and this is what I get for it? Is karma slowing me down? Everything was going so well." How about the storm that comes and floods the road and takes it away? I feel my blessings come and go like that sometimes. Or how about those moments when the state has few resources and the economy is bad, and all that can be done is patch work? You have seen it—road crews shoveling asphalt into holes to hold it over until more can be done.

I used to live with the complications of feeling I had a purpose and I was so lost. My heart used to be so heavy with sorrow, frustration, and anger—I used to wait patiently to get my project on schedule so I could reach my destination. But I have overcome the patch work. I have now secured a great number of resources to keep me moving forward. The awareness of meditation, setting intentions, and believing in the ENERGY around me provides a solid foundation to achieve MY Destiny just as you will.

As I travel the highways in my high-mileage car, I see states that take care of their roads better than others. We humans are the same way; some of us will take care of our Spirit because we know it is important while others will ignore it for different reasons. To continue our soul purpose and desire to accomplish our birth's Journey we ask the societal question: Are we not all Americans? Doesn't every state get the same resources? What is one governor or highway superintendent doing better than the others? The answer is "Nothing really." Sometimes the solution is as simple as prioritizing where you put your resources to get the most out of them, other times it is opportunity and luck, and then again it could be loud cries for change.

Years ago, I petitioned for change and only had half the presentation available to give to God (the superintendent). As I excitedly began working I did not research some of the pitfalls that could occur in my plan for success. I took on employees and allowed them to stay when I knew I had to downsize and change my priorities. In the process, I found partners who were excited about change and were willing to work with me, knowing I had failed in my planning before. They respected my work ethic and attempts to do the right thing even when I should have given up long before.

Earlier we talked about those road construction companies that had bids that just weren't right. This happens to us, too, when we allow others to work for us or against us, and when we are trying to do the right thing. For instance, let's say Kosko Construction lost out to, say, J. Lewis and Company (some East Coast highway construction company). Because Kosko is bigger than J. Lewis and Company, Kosko may try to leverage previous work and sabotage the bidding process or put pressure on officials to award them for future jobs in their voting districts. In contrast, the small firm just wants a fair shot in the project because they feel the main contractor has had enough of the pie and should move over to let someone else in.

The problem with that is that usually the subcontractor is lacking expertise, experience, or information about the processes. I'm not saying they aren't smart enough to figure it out, but perhaps they have never had such a big project, or they are just focused on results but don't understand the importance of quality. How can that be? God would not allow such things to happen, would He? But in fact He does. Every day, someone has an idea on how to do something better than someone else. Does it mean their way is better or what is being done is bad? Not necessarily. It just means any small organization or individual needs to put time into honing their craft.

How do you deal with organizations and God's will when your mind, heart, and soul have other ideas? That answer is different for each of us. What is important today may not be years from now—maybe even tomorrow.

Trust me, I don't want to settle for subcontracting work or live in a state where I feel they are not devoted to change and improvement. But I will evaluate carefully before I commit any further into a verbal or written contract. I have worked with big time players before and left the organization, only to question my thinking: Was the resignation or at-will agreement to let me go better? Did management have more informed information than I did about the needs I had? For a while it seemed great and all was well. But I looked deeper and the message was not as clear as I or they may have hoped.

I started to feel that though the company was committed to me the road map was not right. And as barriers to personal growth appeared they became more or less impatient with my performance. —I gave everything I had to the organization only to feel I had been working out of a dark hole rather than as a partner. The stories are the same: "Come on, we love you and we are doing everything for you, but in return for our loyalty tell us more about what you know about the competition and prove your worth by working harder—longer hours, paying more attention to detail…" Wow! Before you know it, you're wondering What is my status?

Whether we admit it or not, big contracts usually come at a price—and sometimes renegotiations must take place in order to get the players back at the table. Sometimes the process is hostile and in some cases starting from scratch is necessary.

This road project is not for one person alone. You will meet people at some point who have travelled down your path before.

In my opinion, God is like that. He sticks with those that try and he rewards you with, as theBible says, "love without ceasing." All God asks is that we love him and serve him and he will be there for us. Does this mean that nothing bad will happen to us? NO!!! It means if we trust in Him, one day it will get better, and even if it does not we have a place in His home.

Road projects are like that; the road we may want to travel is closed, has detours, or is under construction, but we eventually get to where we want to go. Sometimes we stop in places we've been before; other times, somewhere that is unlikely but along the way. But we always learn something about someone else or ourselves.

Currently, I am under construction and feeling the joy of a big MERGER not only in my Soul's Journey but also in how I accept abundance and how I can now use my increasing resources. I'm not going to promise there won't be delays as you fulfill your life's purpose, but I know for me the one thing that is going to take place is a change of FAITH and HOPE. By setting intentions for all that you desire and pursue on behalf of God and society, you will be on a path of enlightenment that will help you better understand the ROOT of your own past issues and appreciate and invest in those around you who are also seeking the blessing of PURPOSE. Today, I can see why some people are truly labeled a reason, a season, and a lifetime (partner, stranger, etc.). Not everyone will be afforded the aptitude, care, desire, or awareness to serve something higher than their own self-interest.

I don't have a big budget request or worry about name brand equipment but I do need to have competent and trustworthy apprentices, journeymen, and craftsmen (people who are fired up at all levels of following their Life's Cause Journey) around me. God has His plan for me and I am trying to align my plan with HIS as best I can right now. My highways are no longer devastated, and I would be proud to assist others and support their endeavors as others have supported mine "free of will, expectations, and more."

Negative DNA cells (poor examples of family origin) used to attack my roadways, and the storms of manipulation, doubt, and "you can't" used to linger so long in my mind, which affected my actions. I no longer have family of origin or rotten DNA cell depletions as I once did. I no longer allow negative ENERGY or people the ability to take up much space in my mental, emotional, or physical space. No project is perfect and neither am I. Like a safe and reliable highway, I will work on being a solid resource for God's Army. I don't need my name in the papers to say I made a difference. I have the joy in my heart that I am a part of something good. I will contribute the best I can to the effort to bring awareness and Light to those that seek a better way. My contributions may not be enough for some, but at least I give all I can.

Evolution of materials and processes are in everyday life—so it is too for the soul. I am God's highway project.

The month of June, the year 2008, was when I started the project. It is now 2017 and the project is sufficiently funded and supported. One day with the help of my new tribe of Light workers and people seeking their path to fulfill their destiny, we all will find so much excess in our empowerment we can't but want to help others live a more Energetic and fulfilled life. And we will do so though teaching, coaching, and mentoring all who ask for us to share.

Blog Entries
Posted on <u>May 31, 2013</u> by <u>leecsmith1969</u>
<u>Sacagawea</u>

Every journey has a time you encounter different people and even languages, the Question comes when you are asked what is it that you do. Or are asked if you can complete difficult tasks when some possible conflicts arrive.

The Native American who helped Lewis and Clark navigate west of the Mississippi was influential in using her talents to avoid pitfalls with other Native Americans.

So how are we as Americans today so willing to give up many of our rights and just do provisions to not only the wealthy but the supposed government who is guiding us into a "warehouse of forgotten" stuff.

We have lost so many industries and sent away so many jobs, and have the mental meltdown to consider at local, regional, and global levels—tax breaks to those that feel they are above paying taxes or their own share of operational cost just because of greed.

Why are the tax laws so different for small business and "giants"; for instance, Charlotte NASCAR stadium pushing for more breaks or moving the race to Vegas——Phillip Morris or RJ Reynolds moving and/or failing because of more wants. How about banks and other industries moving headquarters from state to state for bigger breaks and more profits?

Why are we having to push Spanish as a second language and we don't even invest in the first? If we go to other countries "English" is the global business language but do not the locals of those countries away from the city center expect us to at least try to learn the language if you would think of living there?

How do you wake up a single-minded individual to see beyond their own walls and comforts? You don't until they hit bottom and even then it is not guaranteed.

For what it is worth "No man is able to do much on their own without some interaction of the other, and no group is successful over others unless there is understanding and agreement upon some idea."

So how can a nation change when people feel they don't have to work together or how does economy change when the groups are not in the same room? A nation once born from ideals of religion has turned into "faith lost" and yet when natural disasters happen and war breaks out or death knocks upon a sick person's door—suddenly the powerful then look for understanding beyond themselves.

The show "Touch" is an amazing look at how we are all connected—which of us care to share the vision?!

Posted on <u>May 22, 2013</u> by <u>leecsmith1969</u>
Inspired Journey

The journey that I share with you today is one that has been traveled well in advance of me. My thoughts, practices, beliefs, and more have all been seeded by those that had belief in humanity, faith in religion, and a sense of moral responsibility to mankind, not of their own successes and accolades of what they have achieved for personal interest.

What happened to being a nation of people and where is free enterprise? We have social programs that have made many dependent. We have lost our sense of direction as a nation, family, and friends. I assure you there are always exceptions but now the majority is those that have forgot how to even write a letter and stand up for corruption and misuse of power.

Over the last 20-plus years we have not stabilized our economy for maximum use of exports and human capabilities. We allow organizations to take tax breaks at the lowest level of government, and yet watch billion dollar profiteers create the "new monopolies" in lower labor and cheap operations.

Unions and the like are no longer effective, nor is a system of government that lobbyists and corporations have so much power to influence market direction and products or unacceptable bills and regulations that are not meant to do anything but create more loopholes for those that can afford to find them.

Our press and entertainment industry has moments of taking on social issues but since news has always made money on the "pain or suffering of others" so too has our last decade of reality shows that are not reality but "embarrassments of people looking for attention."

How do you compete with a global economy when you don't have an education system set up to learn foreign languages in the early school years when it is most effective? Or provide programs based on European or Western civilization that has a global mindset?

Our journey is not about everyone being rich or well off, but we certainly can do better at conserving resources and using better business practices so that we are not paying high costs of living just because we are willing to ignore poor management by people who are determined that "big business" is the only way to go.

We are now a nation of greed, selfishness, and inefficient processes that has allowed the "few" to take advantage of the "many."

Posted on <u>June 30, 2013</u> by <u>leecsmith1969</u>
Church—Loaded Questions Series My Day

Loaded Questions Series-Why did this happen to me?
Matthew 15:21-28

Wow, the message was one that reignited my own spirit—you know that kind of movement that you shiver and say, "Oh! Lord,"

I feel tugging on me! Oh, yes, that is what it is like —twice my spirit let me know that today was a day I was supposed to go to church and hear this message—sure the same message for each of us has a different path...so what was the message of Faith and praise before you have been delivered or granted Jesus and God's blessing for healing or removal from a bad situation?

I know for me I have been in a situation that career wise, and to some degree financially worrying about what is next and yet I am at peace with waiting on my time of blessings. But at the same time—I would love to know what is next. So, for me the message today was that I am on the right path; all I must do is stay the course and continue praising God for what he has done and will do for me even though what is next is not revealed. No matter my question I know I will receive an answer.

Just being here today and knowing the seed of change is upon me—keeps me grounded and hopeful as each day passes. I know what I do alone is not covering all the factors of my faith and social calling but I do believe that for each lesson I pick up along the journey of acceptance in the spiritual Higher Power I will be blessed beyond my own imagination.

The atmosphere is electric, the music alive, and the room captivated by the use of all the things we call comfort today—non-traditional—it was like being at a concert and not worrying about what someone might say about you dancing, waving your hands—what and wearing anything I had in my closet like jeans—I am in—no show or fashion police—just a spiritual good time...

When life puts barriers up—my response like most is asking the question why me? But my response to it makes all the difference—I will study, have faith and overcome—whatever it is—because I believe if I keep my faith Jesus will answer my prayers, while God reveals his plans.

So instead of being bitter because I don't have all the things some have —or any term about covet thy neighbor or feel jealousy—I take pride in knowing my life is not supposed to be like theirs —my path is my path and on that journey my blessings are more than I can ever ask for.

Not only that I got into the car and two more songs followed that sent me smiling down the road—just happy that everything has its timing and its purpose.

Music:
Percy Bady/Canton Jones_ I won't give up.
Wess Morgan_You paid it all.

Posted on July 23, 2013 by leecsmith1969
Template_Model_Copy_Boiler Plate

The Great Degeneration by Niall Ferguson brings about many ideas of why a powerhouse nation has now become the laughingstock of the world. I mean don't get me wrong many countries have their problems but why is it that in the last 50 years, especially the last 20, our nation is now one of greed and self-service—what do we mean by self-service?

The new template is recycling a few bad CEO and leaders, creating recognizable groups, committees, and boards who all agree on maximizing profits and investments for the 1%-10% of the population of wealth owners while the 10% of overachievers manage the workload and marginalize the 90% of the workforce into producing and working for less than what they are worth.

The Model that we have come to accept is deniably wrong—who wants subpar customer service and even less than respect from people who themselves have less than spectacular work ethics. We have become a nation of hiring "those less than us" because our own egos demand we know or feel more important than the person below us—we promote bad habits and ineffective people to ever more responsibility only because we lack the fortitude to do paperwork to admit we hired poorly developed people. We allow poor work and workplace hostility because of the need to avoid confrontation. Have your ever been to a counter and asked for help only to have the clerk look at you like you were bothering them, or how about that manager that thinks they are always right, but has no clue what is going on but they are so happy to wreck the emotional wellbeing of the staff just because they like drama and manipulation?

How can we copy what was good from the world and implement those ideas into a society that still has not and is in denial that race and societal positioning exists?

How is it that the red tape for small businesses and public assistance is so minimal for people born outside the U.S. but those of us born here are looked at as unreliable? We put Indians on reservations and provided a means for every other ethnic group to succeed but yet we have quotas for Blacks, and still judge them on their skin color. Have you seen how much money is made in tanning, beaches and products for Whites to darken their own skin color? Hmm makes you go—so you don't want to be Black because you know there are issues with being seen as "Black" but you don't want to be solely "White" because that is not all in itself attractive? Is there a study done on why people tan on purpose?

If ever I have seen a Boiler plate for failure America is doing it—catering to a small population at the expense of the masses. Not only financially, but morally as well. We have lost what it is like to take care of family, our neighbors, and our coworkers, long gone are family dinners and family time on Saturday and Sunday, taking care of our sick without putting them in a home because it would make our already "so busy day more busy." Imagine an 1855 homesteader telling their grandparents or parents "we will put you in a home because we are too busy building wealth and leading an active lifestyle that if we kept you home we would have to limit our enjoyment!" Really!!!

We use to be a nation of identity but what are we now "reality shows, food networks, and flip this house?" What are our national products? Wal-Mart, Best Buy, Regional all in one gas stops? We can talk about monopolies and a few greedy families, self-serving politicians and ignoring constituents who elect people who have no interests in our wellbeing.

Working in the government was not meant to be a full-time job or catapult us to more riches and power but a public service. How many people would be willing to volunteer time for far meager salaries? If we went back to paying the public servants "insert laugh" just a bus or train ticket, and small stipend for their time; let us say, today's money "50 dollars a day" for only the days they do work, would these same politicians want the job and handle our laws and constitution with such reckless abandon, how about our chief justices and lawyers—all that once had nothing to gain—cut everyone's salary to an eighth of what they have now. Would they not opt for being corporate workers or self-employed?

What if the FDA cut the red tape for new products that have had decent feedback and few side effects, what if we lowered all insurance premiums and reduced the healthcare cost and employee pay to match the shrinking premiums, eliminated and reduced the ease of suing for wrongful injury and negligent actions (so called)—we shut down industries such as tobacco and textile because of false and liable excuses. We sold our labor to foreign countries because we didn't want to pay "fair wages" because we wanted to give executives and owners bigger market shares and profits—we use to make products that lasted and took pride in building things that became monuments to our desires—now we take more shortcuts and use cheaper products while increasing the prices nonetheless.

No matter how you look at it—we are a society lost—super power status gone—AAA bond rating decreased, the dollar useless and national pride-forgotten.

We need new templates and models; we need to copy better means to operate while increasing well known boiler plates for worn out ideas and ideologies.

Posted on <u>September 7, 2013</u> by <u>leecsmith1969</u>
Aptitudes_and One's Love of Life at Work

One's aptitudes (talents) or gifts are found in "1 Corinthians 12," as you seek out those things that not only earn you a living but create wealth in order to define your cultural status or ability to purchase. You at some point, well at least some of us wonder why we are doing the job we have or moving through life using certain skills. Maybe even changing our path because something is eating at us to change.

For instance, I can be proficient with a computer doing "systems administration, or programming" but that is not my ultimate desire, I can plan and respond to emergencies but that in itself is not totally fulfilling either; today, I have found that I/O Psychology is not work and a passion for me. Though I am not in that official role or title of an I/O Psychologist my studies and experiences have allowed me to use those techniques and skills at work.

As I have traveled and moved around the world and semi resettled in the United States I know my spirit is not at rest or prepared at least yet for what I am to become—I get a sense of something bigger and important but not yet blessed to see the seed grow into something purposeful.

God has given me many talents and abilities (Aptitudes). I am not a scripture expert but I do believe the "Good Book" is a guide to living as best we can amongst imperfect people in a world ever changing (some due to our negligence or care). I am consumed by knowledge (seeking) and the desire to share it (wisdom) with others not only about what may be true but planting ideas that may make some search deeper in themselves.

I am a "seeker," a "nomad," one of an old heart and love for what we would call a "reformation or renaissance" of thinking. No subject in itself can be fully explored without looking at other topics and ideas. I love when people give me ideas or share thoughts on things I have yet to explore or read on my own from my limited imagination. So many books turn me on to new subjects and options for new and verifiable or even imaginary information.

All of these things I search out—at some point I use and make examples at work at some point or in some conversation in which I help others seek something they too are unaware. In the end, I am so thankful to God, the Spirits, and those willing enough to open my mind, eyes, and spirit to new things. When I get goose bumps or feel a tear of joy welling up inside me from something so fantastic—nothing but a pure rush or excitement.

Live life as it is never fulfilled and work with passion and use your ability to SOAR!!!!

My father used to say, "You can't soar with the eagles 'eeaarree eeaarree' and whoo whoo with the owls!" Usually in reference to staying up all night and trying to be productive during the day—but I found that my lack of sleep or restlessness is and has been wasted because I am not productive as I could be—so that I have to work on—I will endure and make an effort to smile at the heavens and pay respect to those who failed to repent now in Hell—we are all given the chance to produce and share wonders—or destroy dreams! I choose the light over darkness—may God put his hands upon me and those with a reverent heart—to make our way through and follow our path! He has set before one hair was upon our head.

Aptitudes and Spiritual gifts—What are yours?

Grim Reaper

To me the Grim Reaper Is a fallen angel still at work not necessary to take those who have found the end of their journey but one who partners with those on their journey until the end comes. Representing we are never alone on our walk.

Posted on November 2, 2013 by leecsmith1969

Journal Entry of Self

There are people I always carry with me no matter where I am in the world. When I take time like this some of it is the ability of not being responsible for every decision I make.

Or in simple terms having to be accountable to anyone. I don't know how to settle that part of me—like you I am so independent and have a mind of my own, let's not talk about the various differences of life obligations and things that life enhances or brings down on us.

I prayed in January to have stable living and earnings from good for 5-10 years' minimum. Well! at the moment, that is still not yet happening.

I am not all about money but like you want to be paid a salary for what the perceived worth is at this time. I want to be a millionaire one day not for the lifestyle of the rich and famous but having the option of making a difference and not worrying about paying the bills as I do now.

I look at life like I would a trip made at the last minute—it is based on opportunity and feeling.

For as much fun I have with people—I want to broaden my experiences too—routines are good to a point but I know there is a part of you that just wants to go. Sometimes I feel that I am stuck and not doing as much as I should; however, I could but that is good and bad; overall, it is a balance of my mind and heart being unsettled.

Until I feel that security in my heart I will for some time be a "bucket of experiences; sometimes full, sometimes empty, and sometimes only half full."

I never want anyone to doubt I care, love, and adore them for being themselves, any more than I want to be caged into a small group of we are "robots"—I have seen some great things with people—and have had some great experiences and more to come I hope.

I take these moments of "calendars and expectations" in stride; not to force anyone into a hardship of the mind or heart but one that allows for me to live as God would have it one day. Available to His will, I know some would argue the fact that could be obtained with more time with family and friends and more meaningful involvements, sharing and communication. But sometimes even I get distracted and need time away from everything.

Socially defected is partly who I am—I have learned to be social and maintain some relationships, but I walk a thin cord when it comes to how far I will go and who gets to take the journey—I mean the true journey—one that I am teaching and trying to bring a light of understanding.

Sometimes I want to walk away from everything and hope that God picks me to be the "light" for humanity. But that is not how it works—I have a ton of talent and ability to do a lot of things, and in some sectors, no skill at all. So, what do I want to do to earn millions of dollars, and to get out the rat race? Write books, hope that the job of a lifetime comes that will allow me to begin the savings I look for—taking that experience and opening my own LLC? I don't know.

Technology is nice—and I use it well, but I miss the excitement and wonderment of waiting for the letter in the mail; similar to this writing that tells of the heart. Everything is so fast paced and right now. No matter how we slice it—I tell a few so much that they can't digest it with the understanding and subjectivity it deserves, others get a hint and some days no one gets anything, but what do people truly want? Someone that will act like them on a whim, or planned? When we find someone we like—we want to hide them from the world except when we feel insecure and want to prove to others "someone picked me" —is this all we are? Can't be!

We all have moments we are too busy—but in that it is the mindset that makes the difference—I am secure in who I am most days and to me that is all I need—today.

I don't worry about the words and actions of others— I am a flawed man and have my demons and concerns to live with it; as with my hopes and dreams yet to be availed.

All I ask if I lean too much to one way (objective, subjective, ignorant, or proud) let me know—but if I live within reason, don't doubt my sincerity—I won't doubt you! I can't be the same for everyone (a lot of hats to wear, but I was created this way); you are you. Is that so bad to you? And all the other things around any of us, what is most important? So many people that swirl around the lake of distrust, insecurity, pain, and selfish gain; can't we break free and find solace in knowing those that aren't like us make us stronger?—then let's take the best of that and be content to grow those few things then endure; over the hard labor of growing weeds around our minds and hearts; and plant seeds of success, support, and gratitude—the kind of things that make us grow.

Well I hope I didn't bore you with this—but since I had to touch on me, and how I feel; I just wanted to share where my head is today.

"I am mad that I am not able to see what I am supposed to be doing, happy that God did give me the mind to move around, sorry for those that don't see the true me, happy that the few that do let me be me, hurt that I can't make the difference I want to today, glad that I still have breathe to Today, mad that I can't seem to get far enough ahead to sustain the living I feel I earned, and happy that I have not ended up on the street or dead, hurt because I am judged harshly and misunderstood, but glad I can control my emotions not to respond to the criticisms I don't deserve, disgraced because I have less than I want, but happy I have what I need; tormented because I don't know what is expected from me from God, but willing to take on the challenge when it comes; hurt that I have to depend on others at times, but blessed that when I need help it is there; lost and confused because I feel I should not have to endure one more failure or disappointment; but glad that those experiences help me help others; lonely at times because those I want to know me, ignore me; but glad that on the good days they accept me; tired of fighting for what I can't see, but glad I have a fire still in me to take another step; screaming to be accepted in a world that could care less by a majority of people who care only for themselves, but so glad I have the mind to know what they don't; frustrated being on the outside too often, but glad to know I can view all the sources; saddened by the fact my journey is one of a loner, but honored I can relate to others; grief filled by so much I have yet to understand, but humbled that I know it."

Well enough about me today—I wonder how my rating is overall if a survey was done by strangers and those that are close to me? Fit in, oddball, stranger, freak, who knows—but this is just a small part of my obligations to keep living because I feel the fire of making a difference, and the burden for not accepting what is; rather than just accepting this is all you will be.

Posted on June 23, 2013 by leecsmith1969

From My Window

From my window, I can dream of a simpler life where money and power were only a passing for tyrants. That life where families would work together and friends were true.

I look through the forest in my backyard and see a path barely visible leading to a pond. I know today I won't walk out to see it; I'll not interrupt the dead leaves of winter or rustle any little animal's slumber. But I hope to get down there when the spring warmth comes. I see children playing now; with no care in the world—they are equal. No prejudice and shame about them. Unlike their elders who struggle with dreams gone! Somewhere reads, "Give me your tired, your poor, your huddled masses…" "…that all Men are created equal."

The sun is falling below the trees now bringing light into the room. Life has a way of changing our dreams and ambitions (from innocence to self-adulation) but as I look out my window and see the branches blowing in the breeze, I listen to the children's innocent laughter. And I gain some hope that as the days continue "We the people" will one day truly stand together and know we are all free.

But till that day "every man, woman, and child" are treated equally I will look out from my window and pray for better days.

From my window innocence is true and unwavering, in my heart is hope and sadness, but in my dreams is an alternate reality, one that sees everyone as equals. From my window, I can dream, hope, pray, and ponder and now I sit smiling… From my window…

So, the question is why do we still have issues with race and equality? How do you put it aside when finance and status are still limited in fields of employment in areas where groups of people are massed in small areas and the resources controlled by groups, corporations, families, or just plain ignorance of those complaining and supposedly looking to increase their own position in life?

I can only hope to see more diversity in all things but we were not meant to live in a world equal, the same, or where we have the same morals and character for people and society—nor can we speak the same language and take away the same meanings.

From my window—I ponder a better world—how can I influence my sector of influence—this is my journey to find the answer.

Posted on <u>June 9, 2013</u> by <u>leecsmith1969</u>
Journey of a Sage To Be

There are a lot of visions, hopes, and faith to be revealed to everyone; however, those revelations and interpersonal moments of growth only come when time, maturity, self-awareness, and acceptance become a part of your everyday outlook.

Not all of us want to be so socially, globally, or self-enlightened; nor seek that higher consciousness that comes with the joy or pain of knowing the good, bad, or deceptive nature of man's selfish nature. Because that would mean they would have to change themselves and their own belief systems; many individuals are fine with the layers of "societal norms"; love, work, family, and individual success. But is that all there is to life?

We know that answer is NO! Well maybe some of us more than others.

So, what is it we are afraid of? Being alone, dying, being left behind, not fitting in, or just plain having to deal with our own self. Any combination of variables makes us who we are and tends to either validate or discredit our systems of belief. So how do we cope with things that make us uncomfortable? Are we to always think our opinion alone is correct? What arguments do we feel acceptable and which do we tend to reject?

I am a self-proclaimed Nomadic-Renaissance Man; I have been blessed to learn and experience that most have not. I have taken some teachings, advice, and assumptions from different people young and old. Though I have disagreed with some ideas; others I have accepted. When we are born to a locale, we have a choice to migrate within limits or we break them and expand our borders; with that being a simple analogy of travel: are our minds not the same? Can we be local or regionally minded individuals who migrate and travel beyond borders and space yet maintain as non-believers of global decisions or even history for that matter?

Can we continue to be global travelers and still ignore cultural differences outside our own country or understanding about international affairs? Are our schemas and prejudices so hard to get over; and if we can lessen how we respond to our surroundings then could we not be better interpreters to human irrational thinking, actions, etc.? No one person's intelligence or foresight is better but can what we understand about imagination and dreams affect our daily interactions for acceptance, dreams, assumptions, etc.? These are but a few questions for you to ponder.

I don't know nearly as much as I have the capacity to; yet, I choose and am prepared to broaden my belief systems by learning of other cultures and topics that were not given to me as a child or young adult. I have found that I am more interested in heightened awareness of an individual, personal spirits, religion, global news, and such rather than the essence of love and preconceived notions of traditional man and woman relationships. How many times do we divorce, split, and exit what we initially considered significant relationships? Not everyone is comfortable with being alone—true in some cases but shouldn't we study, challenge, and process our interpersonal challenges and gifts before reinvesting in someone new? There are plenty of negative influences that affect us (i.e. billboards, friends & family, pessimistic & mean people, and let's not forget the gossip and the lure of drama).

Don't get me wrong. A relationship can be a jewel of life but negative energy can be an issue if the sharing partner is afraid of interpersonal challenges. How that partner deals with anger, oppression, conflict, or hurt feelings helps decide if the relationship is uplifting or one that drags you down. I am a natural loner or person willing to go for some time on his own to sort out the issues of resolving and determining what is my issue with past relationship history, love, and duty that affect my ability to be a positive influence or accept positive influences. My family had its own issues that affect my point of view of relationships and those I spent time in that did not work. I am also seeing and living with bigotry, hatred, low self-esteem, victimhood, and other self-destructive behaviors not only in my family but people I have met in my life. My experiences and others' have affected my outlook on life and my world views; however, I continually work at learning and improving my intellectual freedoms so that I can respond slower to some situations and quicker to those that I did not before.

I have never subscribed to many traditions such as holidays, birthdays, family events, school, etc. However, there have been some great events I have taken part in. I have never thought of what fitness meant to me until I was a young adult but I have been a part of some exercise program or sport all my life. There is a link between mind and body and the confidence one has when others appreciate the outer shell (face, body type, voice, or some other attraction); however, have you ever thought about the people you hang with and how you feel about yourself — are your interpretations good or bad depending on what you see in the mirror or consciously think of yourself?

Out of the issues of personal self, family & friends, pessimistic people & media; it is understandable people have issues with being positive and enjoying life, relationships, and more. How does work fit in to all these assumptions and attitudes? What you love your job but dislike the people, management, and work ethics of co-workers, etc. Daily interactions and progress to be a positive influence is or can be altered. Have you ever had great news and when you went to share a spouse, friend, or companion stops you because they want to tell you how awful their day was; of course you have and sharing your news is off the table right? Well, such things happen—your good day may be someone else's stress or depressed day and vice versa. But with good communication, sympathy, empathy, and more each of you could be able to share different views, feelings, and more. However, this is not guaranteed.

The Bible, philosophers, scholars, ordinary people have concluded that it is our own human nature that can be a positive or negative influence. There are things in the environment that make people feel as if they are a victim but ultimately that is not all true because as a human being we have the choice to change our external environments and our internal attitudes towards those things we do not like.

In the end, it is of our own fortitude that we can embrace God's ultimate design or struggle against Karma and life's ultimate path that every man and woman must experience; remember what works for another may not work for you, each of us have minds that channel ideas and knowledge a different way. Only when we accept our own spark to life can we find the true joy that is within us and in others.

There is a long way to go on this journey of life but if you are afforded even the slightest joy of companionship embrace it because right then there is nothing more fashionable than where you are. Greed, wrath, sloth, pride, lust, envy, gluttony are all proposed sins that are detested; judge not for you will be judged yourself.

Evolving Beliefs
Love and Its Sensitivity

What kind of man am I? One that looks at life with a different view as to that of love and living; I was watching the Netflix original show "House of Cards" and in it or shall I say throughout the show, the main characters of the Underwoods have a unique and sometimes complicated but simple relationship. I can assure you if you have seen the show—at first glance you might think wow, they support each other and are truly in love and have this thing figured out. To the outside they are but normal. However, well I won't spoil the plot. At any rate, what struck me tonight was the fact that there was a line or two that dealt with trust and communication.

In both these, the Underwoods have worked very hard to make this the staple of their marriage as to reduce undue stress; however, there have been a couple of instances this has failed but they work through it. So why am I writing this today? Maybe for me it is a learning or teaching point or maybe even a reminder how I enjoy life and it is not on anyone's terms but those that are right in front of me and those around me. We all have a perception of what our happy is. In the show episode 6 season one, on his death bed, the dying bodyguard to the congressman's family told Claire Underwood he hated her husband and he took pride in his work because of her—her voice, or seeing her—and how he felt Mr. Underwood underappreciated her. Mrs. Underwood replied with a story of when Mr. Underwood proposed, "...Claire if you marry me just because you want to be happy say no, but if you never want to be bored say yes." She then went on to touch the dying man's manhood and said, "Is this what you wanted?" He replied, "Please stop." She said, "You gave me your truth now you have mine."

At the end of the show Mr. and Mrs. Underwood with some…. went upstairs and the credits rolled.

So why do I invite this conversation or thought—well that is just me—always inspired by the weirdest things. I have been told I should respond in certain ways I guess in my time to how someone else perceived their view on some situation and/or reacted based on how they might themselves hope they would if they were affected or otherwise engaged.

I write this because the whole of the show is pseudo-reality life and how people use, barter, lie, commit, defend, chase, aspire, crash, "go along with the heard or become lions!"

"I love being in love, but I also love other things, like not being jealous, overly sensitive, or needy." — Dark Jar Tin Zoo

Over the past couple of years, I have found something so simple in myself and I love it. It is amazing the things you learn about yourself when you walk away from the wrong people and find those more suited to who you are. Now the question is what is next. I don't know but I do know boredom is not it. I love life, I love people, I love my God, and I love having hope and faith that if I keep trying to let this vessel I have on earth serve a higher purpose, I will see the "Kingdom of God."

Don't let others skew your perceptions because they want you to be like them. Which part of them would you want to be—no clue? Me either—I do know something drove me to write this— no other reason than to share my joy—love and loving is so great a gift, and it comes in so many packages. How do you see your love packaged?

If it were given to you in a box, what do you see? How would it look, how would it feel, would it have a scent? If you had to exchange love "boxes with your lover" what do you imagine that exchange being, how would you respond if the box was bigger or smaller than your own? What if what was inside didn't fit your mood, or perception; would you still laugh, live, and love? Would you hug or kiss, or more!

"'You will never be bored,' he said" as she walked away from the dying man she said to him about her husband, "He knew I didn't want to hear the same lines others had proposed and there were many." She continued, "My husband knew me and knew what I needed."

That is powerful, so many opportunities and in the end, there was that man who saw something in her that was different and he took the opportunity and went for it. She liked that about Mr. Underwood; he went after what he wanted.

So here we are—what is it in life you are after, will you go for it in the herd or will you make your own path?

There is beauty in old Shells, as we look at an old home; we question what was it like then; What could it be tomorrow? (Do it yourself project (DIY) or other renovation project) These images are about possibilities! The journey is about questioning when we are broken, how we mend, then recover, and grow to use all those experiences to See Beyond! And enjoy the universal blessings.

Dream without Fear and Love without Limits!

I like that saying I'm not sure where it started but it is a good line. I smile as I write these words, wondering what thought random strangers might have of those that say they love me; family, friends, those that one day too will read my books.

I stand because I have something brewing in me. I can't even understand. I move forward because my destiny is in front of me. I love and share my life with those whom I cross paths. "Not even looking, we find," and sometimes those are the greatest gifts. Some random smile, eye contact, or kind word makes the difference not only to the one who made the gesture but those who receive it and those that witness it. Do you have a story from when someone told you, "Something is different about you. Did you cut your hair, lose weight?" Was it most likely love or the gesture of it?"

Well, ponder away and smile—take notes, write a letter to someone you have been wanting to write for some time—AA tells recovering alcoholics to write those or call those they have hurt or offended. Why not do the same for someone you love or care for?

Good night! To those who are willing to expand their minds and open their hearts and believe, take a chance. Look out. What do you see?

The Article

I came across an article that certainly "stirred" some thoughts and I wanted to share. You have heard of the statement "Woulda, Coulda, Shoulda"? The article had to do with letting things go and regrets we might have throughout our course in life. The following are thoughts that were brought out that give us things to think about:

Dwelling on past mistakes or missed opportunities consumes one's ability to enjoy the present. Letting go of regrets is a process—it's not a one-time event. Studies of people with a neurological inability to experience regret show just how essential this mental skill is. Without regret, basic decision-making and social skills are severely impaired. There is a value in negative emotions. Regret is useful for signaling to people that it is time to change their strategy. If you are reflecting/meditating on how things could have been better that's not good, but a sharp, rapid emotional response followed by a behavioral change, followed by the disappearance of the emotion, that is perfectly good for us. (Do you agree?) In other words, regret—and our desire to avoid it—is a major part of healthy living. Regrets are an indicator that our brain is trying its best to guide us through a complicated social environment. Regret is all but universal, spanning age and culture in its agonizing variations. For every choice, we make—good and bad—a numberless multitude of options are left untried, each one an opportunity to second-guess, brood, and ask yourself the perilous question: What if?

Researchers have noticed age-related distinctions in how and why we experience regret. The young are more likely to regret things they did rather than things they did not do. After all, at that stage in life there is still time to see Australia, write a novel, etc. But as we age this tendency reverses, and it is what you did not do that stings. The sense of loss can be devastating. How we respond to regret depends on several factors including our ability to correct whatever we did (or did not do) wrong. It is the element of control that makes the regret powerful. If you can fix it, the negative emotions, especially regret, tend to be stronger and longer lasting. If you cannot fix it, something in our brain kicks in and shuts it down (this is a good thing).

There is a term called the **paradox of choice**—the more choices we have, whether in television or career, the greater the likelihood we will be dissatisfied with the results. Applying the model to life decisions, a mild case of buyer's remorse becomes a major source of life regret. In a world where there are an almost infinite number of choices, the number of things you could have done will be much greater.

In a culture that celebrates stick-to-itiveness, learning how to throw in the towel is hardly second nature. But according to the many questionnaire-based studies, "redirecting life goals" is a function of healthy aging. Funneling time, effort, and emotional energy into the pursuit of a lost cause can lead to depression and illness. It may seem counterintuitive, but in truly hopeless situations, it is healthier to simply admit that things are out of your hands.

As people age, they take into account the amount of time they have left. When time is perceived as being constrained, people tend to pursue goals related to feeling states that pay off in the moment. There is a prediction that even the ME Generation will navigate the golden years in the traditional fashion, gradually adjusting goals to accommodate the time they have left. People will be motivated to accept the choices they make in order to achieve happiness.

What did you think about my discussion paper? I really enjoy reading articles, books, etc. that give me information that allow me to examine my life and bring other perspectives to light.

Knowledge is so important to a conversation. I always think about how objective statements are made because they are backed by educated research and thoughtful consideration; subjective statements mostly come from uninformed and emotional reactions. Which do you use to support your ideas?

Friar Westbrook
Enlightenment from Within—A Responsible Change

As a writer, it is my responsibility to share thoughts and dreams, and to illustrate words in such a way to make people feel. There are stories, poems, and other literature that each of us find great, offensive, lacking depth, and so forth. A few years ago, I tried to find as many of my works as possible and put them into manuscript form. Though unpublished, I shared my life's work up to that point with many people. That first work was an example of the various stages of my life and my thoughts as I saw them through poems and in some cases short stories. This particular work will be the beginning of a few chapters that has been in the works for years, and that is my search for enlightenment.

Chapter 1—Choices

For years, I have invited good and not so good people into my life; and in those same instances I have found some very good acquaintances, friends, lovers, and forgotten. I have lost more than I have acquired in my lifetime but I have been blessed beyond my expectations and favored when I should not have been. I allowed ignorance to claim my life and it has cost me relationships, jobs, and self-worth. I have had strained relationships with my siblings, my parents, and those that have loved me or at least wanted me in their life.

Some time ago I fell away from the church only to find myself walking back into it one dark evening. That set events in motion for me to return to the U.S. and start my life over. Since returning I have spent an enormous amount of time in school and looking for meaningful employment. I have allowed myself on more than one occasion to deal with my demons (named adultery and seclusion). Thank God I don't drink or do drugs; I would have been really in bad shape. The hardest thing anyone has to contend with is their flaws and failings. Mine have been adultery and seclusion. I don't remember the instant I became an adulterer but I did. My sin of the flesh has cost me a lot in time, love, faith, trust, and my own self-worth. This sin not born of my own consciousness but something—I tried and try to rationalize it as something society placed upon me, even those very women I encountered. However, no matter the instance or catalyst, I choose to enter a relationship. I might not have if I were more controlled, faithful, etc. I have to the best of my knowledge not purposely hurt anyone knowingly but I know I hurt some and destroyed their impression of me in the process. To you, I am sorry. To those I will never get to say it to or share this with I am sorry to you as well. To my fault, seclusion is my escape from my sins and the life I don't have that I want today, yesterday, and tomorrow. I find enjoyment in seclusion even when I am by all means a gentleman, a good father, partner, etc. I find seclusion to be my spring of energy when I am not tending to flocks of people who want, need, or desire my attention. It is hard for many people to understand why I would want to be alone when they themselves could offer warmth and hospitality. I don't need what others do—not for the most part. I am secure in my presence, ability, and independence.

I find the pull to make right those habits and trends that have plagued my time, my resources, and rendered me from obtaining the grace, love, support, and blessings meant for me by Christ. I have some very good friends, associates, acquaintances, and family supporting my basic survival as I have been unemployed for over two years. My military obligation in the reserves has benefited me as well when it comes to meeting some of my basic needs.

In addition, regardless of all the faults and worse conditions, I remain favored, determined, and supported, not only from those that want nothing but with sincere friendships and hope for another human being and belief in the humanity of man, knowing that not all men and women are equal or receive equal compensation, etc. God has not let me fall but so far. With such a long layoff (tears)—choked up—could be worse off than I am today. Thank you (looking up) —Thank you!

Chapter 2—Biased

Over the last two years I have been exposed to the highest level of bias and prejudice I have ever witnessed in my life. I have been run off the road with friends and family in a car and nothing was done about it. I have been fighting with agencies over identity theft and nothing is settled completely. I have been passed over for jobs because of my color, ethnicity, and gender. I have been terminated on false grounds of ability and adaptability. I have been given lower wages than peers who have had lesser backgrounds and education. I have been denied promotions because of background, color, and race. I have been rightfully and unjustly biased against by those women I have been honest and forward with. There are times you have sinned and not been caught but are assumed to have done so anyway. And when it has been justified, never fully being forgiven. When that happens, it is time to move on. I truly believe if you have made every effort to say I am sorry and changed a behavior that action is resolved and should be left out of future disagreements. But we are human and it is easier to look at past achievements (good and bad) and fail to achieve happiness if we focus on those feelings that we feel now. For example, telling someone you're disappointed because they didn't call you is harmful and usually will create guards in the other person, but saying you are disappointed because you wanted to hear from them is not as harsh and is more informative as to how you are feeling inside rather than towards the other. Don't get me wrong I have abused and have been quick to determine (find bias) in someone in a few words or on actions I did not feel appropriate. But I do try to take more time now to carefully approach and reply to others.

Chapter 3—Determined

Several years ago, I found I had failed in controlling (no excuses) my sin for adultery and my need to be alone—nomadic behavior (my demon-seclusion). However, not until a year ago did I decide I was not the man I should be and asked for forgiveness and the opportunity to change who I was. Since then I have done a lot of changing, with moments of indecision and in some cases "falling off the wagon" —failing to improve habits that I know are wrong. I have and will continue to find the "me" I want to be. I have gotten the courage a long time ago to say "no" and "no more." And as I find peace in those few kind souls, my family, friends, and strangers, I will change the path that I have been placed upon—the path of overgrowth; underbrush, thorns, marsh, and thickets. I will find my way to a better clearing that has respect, love, kindness, and soft words towards not only others but me. I want the new path, cleared of and void of despair, pain, and disappointment. In my head, I see either mountains of sand leading to an oasis or some wide path through the woods with lavish flowers, trees, and beauty.

I won't get to the "enlightenment" today but I am determined that getting rid of old habits, distractions, and unhealthy friendships is necessary. Everyone knows that if you are not on the same path, trouble ensues. To stop that from happening any longer I am to take care of me, my family, and those that offer and truly abide by the belief "do for others without expectation." Anything else is a lie I no longer want to live or tolerate in my life. Simplicity is my goal, and that is one goal I intend to seek. I have a mission and goal (forward thinking) for myself and that is to be a better parent, partner, brother, son, leader, and figure not only in my heart but in my family's name, God's eyes, and in the end those that get to walk the path of change and enlightenment with me. This is a continual process, not the beginning and never ending. Stay tuned. There are more chapters to come.

A Wonderful World To Be In Destination Unknown

Over the last couple of months, I have had the pleasure of seeing quite a bit of history in Jordan, and I hope that more will come. Some weeks ago, I got to witness seeing Pope Francis in a stadium in Jordan. Throughout the event, which was done in Latin and Arabic, a couple songs hit a chord. I took the sacrament and enjoyed the surroundings. At one point I felt my spirit shiver from within, a sign of good things as the choir sung Hallelujah.

Then, I was already reading a book called The Untethered Soul, and a book of Angels, along with Fallen Angels, and Hearing God's Voice. The first two were about looking inside to the spirit you feel and using that memory of time past and God spirit to improve your intuition of the things around you. A couple other books on the psychic self also aid in meditating and trusting the inner voice that is given to you to navigate through life and see things around you.

As I started getting more into the books, I took a trip to Anjara to visit an orphanage (Lady of the Mount). However, before getting there, I stopped at a Roman ruin in the town of Jerash on the way. What a view! The columns that still stood were one of the largest sites I have seen to date—more so than Greece at this time. It was amazing. The things good craftsmanship lends itself to in history! Well, on to the orphanage.

The teen boys there were so happy and well-mannered which is a sign of a good home. A colleague (male) and I played basketball and helped the boys with doing flips on the mattresses. At the end of the day it was good though I did at one point take a knee to the chin. We ate and had laughs. As we began to leave I found out the sanctuary housed the statue of the Virgin Mary holding Jesus as a child. In May 2010, the statue cried blood and was validated a miracle. What an awesome moment for those witnesses. All I can say is what a surprise on that day. Thank God for allowing me the opportunity to see such sights so unexpectedly.

So here I am on my latest find in the books I currently am reading. I have had a great opportunity to talk to a good group of Arab men from various countries and with that had an opportunity to learn a few phrases in Arabic and some of the culture, even rereading the Quran and sharing ideas on life and religion.

My latest find while reading the book Fallen Angels was the information on The Council of Nicaea, convened by the emperor Constantine, which decided which books would be handed to the people, as well as the creation of the Nicene Creed. Another find on the Nag Hammandi texts—Gnostics—"knowledge." Oh, the things yet to be discovered as God and Jesus would have wanted it. My spirit soars with the thought of getting closer to the higher awareness that was meant for you. Well, for now this ends this chapter but I can only imagine the things yet to be revealed.

I love the Journey even though I don't know the destination.

New Ideas
The Mantra

The Optimist Creed

Promise Yourself—

To be so strong that nothing can disturb your peace of mind.

To talk health, happiness and prosperity to every person you meet.

To make all your friends feel that there is something in them.

To look at the sunny side of everything and make your optimism come true.

To think only of the best, to work only for the best, and to expect only the best.

To be just as enthusiastic about the success of others as you are about your own.

To forget the mistakes of the past and press on to the greater achievements of the future.

To wear a cheerful countenance at all times and give every living creature you meet a smile.

To give so much time to the improvement of yourself that you have no time to criticize others.

To be too large for worry, too noble for anger, too strong for fear, and too happy to permit the presence of trouble.

LIFE IN POEMS

Moving to the
Universe's Energy

The Poet

Aligning with the Power of the Creator
**The Need to Balance your Chakras
through Meditation and Prayer**

Hears My Prayer

*God here's my prayer— please hear me
Give me that love I seek and let me return it fully
Let me stand true, dear and most of all do till our time ends on earth
Give me what I have refused to accept and let
what I have to give blossom fully.
Let me see the path ahead— and give me wisdom to follow wisely
Forever this and more*

My Prayer to God

Oh! Lord how I follow you faithfully and believe in your ethics I ask of your serene wisdom without clouds and fog, I pray for joy and happiness, not only for me but others—I have gifts like no other and I don't know what or where they lead to! I have a time of my life where I'm at peace within. With my morals and ethics—however I feel alone even amongst others—I've missed love and true feelings—and even refused love when it came freely—I want perfection that I measure to be true— but know that's not reality so I ask you God—create moments that remind me of joyous times past and future dreams to come—Lead me with patience, give me wisdom to understand nature (earth life) and wisdom to achieve your ultimate glory. These things I ask sincerely.
AMEN

My Prayer for Understanding

Lord, I ask of your patience and forgiveness for all I've sinned and misunderstood.
In my heart, I know I've a purpose. You guide me in pieces, which I see, but my unsteady mind pleas for knowledge that I don't understand—yet. Guide me patiently because my steps aren't sure and my path unclear—I will follow bravely and sure in Your care—Every day I ask for guidance—but I know it comes when Your Ready-Lord—my human self fails undoubtedly often—with every failure comes knowledge—give me the strength—give me the strength to teach and learn from others the way You want us to live. May you bless me to give to others as they have given to freely to me. May my many thanks to God be heard—?
And in this imperfect world may you give me an aide to love and cherish as we thrive to do Your work: may You give me wisdom to follow You and lead those to who need Your many Blessings.

My Prayer of and for Righteous Use

Use me Lord as you see fit and guide me
See the true light—I ask to do your will freely in my own accord.
I allowed myself to become victim to the same mistakes more than once.
I ask that now you help me learn from those falls.
Use my given ability to help others, let me feel your grace as I carry out your work.
Use me Lord to give back and to enjoy such tasks.
Give me the strength to share my knowledge, creativity, and vitality with those who currently have lost their own vigor for or in life.
Use me, guide me, teach me, love me and never forget me.
All that I ask of you Lord, may you bless me with the skills and knowledge to share it with others.
Use me as a mediator between your almighty teaching and this world's trials—bless me with the wisdom to see your daily work as a triumph among our people.
Teach me to be a righteous man: Use me to all that you've allowed me to be.
You have a task, a peak for me to climb as I search and work for your blessing...
Give me the will to have the faith to endure.
I am asking to be put to a Righteous Use!

My prayer for forgiveness: Tears won't fall but the frustration hurts

As he sits by the open window and thinks about what should have been a moment of bliss
He finds that interpretation is lost by technology
What has the world come to? —we all have feelings to safeguard—
each of us have a past we sometimes don't want known or want to relive

My God why is this happening—can I not find happiness too—whether it be alone to wander the earth only living in temporary bliss —has it to end now—it sure feels like things are mounting and I don't know how to stop them

My goodness I look at her and I want more but I can't have it—I am not confused about where I am —I know it is something I don't want but yet I am here because it allows me not to live with anyone else —drama—maybe I was wrong—

By not being free I am never without it—but what about the past, are we not to look past it—can we ever grown from it. I was told I through history into the present—and yet I feel at every turn I am being judged not only by my own mistakes but those of others—how much good can come of tragedy?

I feel so tired—and hurt—my eyes seem to swell but nothing falls—but I feel that shouting will do me no good—I have no friends that I can tell everything to Lord only you—my peers, family, and those that say they love me—judge me—I can't escape the pain—give, give, give you say and turn the other cheek. Jesus died for all sins and we are so petty not to forgive one—Lord I am a sinner—adultery is my crime—I didn't ask for this and yet I am here—please hear me—save me from the torment I placed on myself.

Forgive me for trying to live the life of imperfection in a world that thinks "my way is better"—I hear nothing anymore—and every day that passes I feel a little less—I see fewer hopes of happiness—I am lost now—pushed back into my reality—I am alone—I am a NOMAD—meant to wander—knowing only brief happiness—because I have lost my faith in humanity and yet I want to save it, I feel no love because giving it comes with heartache, I have no friend that will let me be me, I can count on strangers but knowing they will never want to know me.

I am forsaken but I will not let the devil have me—as the breeze blows through the window—I sit frustrated thinking is it time to walk away from it all? Where will I go, what will I do, I have nothing —stripped of all things that make me a part of society—except a card and a passport but even in my own country I am not wanted—I am no beggar, poor, or destitute man—but yet I have nothing—no ties, nothing—I am no better than those that look at me with different eyes. I am a man taking up space but looked upon as a void—they love me—but doubt me so—how can that add value—trust and hope.

My fears are not of being alone but having contributed nothing of essence in this life—forgive me Lord—may you take me and this pain—make me new—make me whole—place me in your care—because today—the tears are there but nothing will fall—the frustration is gone now—but I am left walking empty—I need a miracle, joy, a blessing something to let me know I am still your child. Watch over those that would watch over me—may those I hurt find solace—I am on bended knee asking forgiveness and to those that want me harm—may they know I sit at Your alter, wishing them well.

I end here Lord weeping—tears that won't fall-My prayer for forgiveness

In Thought

While alone in thy own setting many thoughts come about thee.
But Thou side thoughts still fall upon thee.
But what's so strange enough while sitting alone thoughts of past, present, future pass before thine eye.
Questions of thou own life from times past nag and bother thy own mind.
Assumptions of relations gone tend to stress 'n one's decision on mentally directed cares.
In times past thine eyes have seen abuse, mentally, physically and morally.
Thine's ears have been told about famine unwants, famine injustice, famine distrust, but no matter what thou eyes, ears, or mouth witness.
Things of days gone turn up to brandish memory's rather forgotten (wanted).
But all in all, the mind has many answers that only the body owner can dredge and
Form a decision.
Yes, another mind can give hints but in the end, thou has the last voice.

There's so much to learn so much to pass on.
But what's even more at play is feelings of trust and loyalty.
For one to believe one must believe in self, the same holds true trust and loyalty.

> *These things and more come from*
> *In Thought*

Patches such as Life!

Whatever is has already been, and what will be has been before; and God will call the past to account. Ecclesiastes 3:15

I have seen something else under the sun:

The race is not to the swift of the battle to the strong, nor does food come to the wise or wealth to the brilliant or favor to the learned; but time and chance happened to them all.

Have you ever dreamt a dream and seen it before: even though you know you'd not been there—***Déjà Vu!***

Do you remember being awake and well active, found yourself asking the air, "I've seen this before" — ***Premonition!***

Have you done all that you can to satisfy yourself while on earth? Have you ever asked why good and bad events happened to you? ***Destiny!***

Have you or someone else foretold your future in God's plan? ***Prophecy!***

Have you noticed how there is no clear answer to all of life: with all the sources and people who contain the information— all their wisdom is limited? Why? ***Imperfect Man!***

I don't know the source of my writing or why I write lies in front of me, but whether it is passion or direction my hand scribes what you see; What are the words meaning? I say to you it depends on your own interpretation. ***Gifted!***

What you've glanced over are just some of what I call the

> *Patches such as **Life!***

Something Within

To cross the treacherous waters that may have failed to pass:
To fly through the air as a Bird;
To blow across the land as a high Wind;
But NO! I am human my spirit requires a different Fire or
feeding—that words can't describe.
That thing that guides me is only voiced from within—But it
gives Hope and Strength:
That gift of something unknown makes me Who I Am!

My Path to Take

I have seen many things and know not much of any
I have been given a gift that cannot be explained
I can travel the road less traveled but find the path long
I have never been a follower only a leader
I have loved and shared much but now I am guarded
I chose to do wrong over right in instances, but believe in good
No one knows but he how I will end up and he is not saying
I know what to do but will I when the times comes
Nevermore sung the raven, Nevermore….
The trees are thick in front of me and there are footpaths in three
directions.
I am the one in control of my own…. It is my path to take.
Wissen Schaft (Learning) as you go!

To live a life of travel is what some people thrive for and so do I.
While in my travels I have learned, C'est a' dire (That is to say) from
being in France. While traveling one learns many phrases such as
Wie Geht's? German for How goes it? Just being in Germany is
Wunderbar (Wonderful) because you meet new people and learn
about their culture. En ami (as a friend) I suggest you visit at least

one country in your life but if you never get the chance or if you just don't want to C'est la Vie, French for That's Life!

Today, if asked, How do you feel? I would say what a Frenchmen might say Comme si, comme ca, (so-so).

Back to traveling, you might have a better time if Ju amie ist au mieux! (If your friend is on intimate terms) then you can have many memories down the road, if you're new to each other that is very exciting as well.

But single or with someone traveling brings great Volupti (pleasure) to self and others.

Hoping that you get out and explore new sights!!!

I will leave you with one more saying: Voila Jout (That's All)

Mystic

Something enigmatic, mysterious or of the occult in religious sect
Something such as worldly unknowns may be called Mystic
  What you ask —
  The rebirth of God's son
  The building of the pyramids
  The gift of super intelligence (geniuses)
 The sudden depletions of civilizations past
   Why -----
Possibly ------
   When --------
  Times long past
  Present secrets yet unveiled
  Future finds waiting on old selects
   MYSTIC
   Yet many finds
  Many self-explanations
  But still so many things are
   MYSTIC

Theories

Theory of Evolution
Theory of Man
Theory of Survival of the Fittest
Development of the Atom
Invention of Light
Discovery of Electricity
Exploration of the Sea
The study of Astronomy
The development of ancient cities, and works past
Wonders of the World
All of this and more to come—
How? Why? Who? and What?
But understanding — Why do so many simple instruments—and
inventions seem so simple, but yet one like yourself and I
can't explain it whether true or not
        THEORIES

Things to learn from

        Follow my words, not my examples
Follow or lead, but follow behind me
        Speak softly, and even speak softly when you must be firm
Speak kindly, even when you must say NO
        Learn to understand that EXPERIENCES are
Those Things to Learn form!

No Man is Totally Free!?

    Have you read your constitution and its bylaws? It tells you outright
No Man can have all rights expressed without invading another's—so tell
me are you totally Free?

How do you make a living? Do you know how the money you never see is being spent? How is it to work so hard and not receive all your earnings? Tell, me if you could make a choice what would you make?

Did you know any institution is one that you lose your individualism? Of course, not, who wants to think of themselves as a prisoner, or slave to industry or a large institution. You say you're not held or bond against your will—WRONG you are in uniforms, dress codes. Try coming to your job late, leaving early, taking extreme lunches, walking out when you're Mad—Come on tell me now —is any man totally free?

How about closer to home—can you do everything you want? How about the land you rent or own? Can you totally run someone's life, wife, children, parents and Friends—Do they do everything you ask or say? I don't think so! So, tell me are you totally free?

Can you drive a car, ride a bike, walk on the street or use public transportation any way you want—Now you get the picture... There are rules and regulations... I tell you we weren't all given our place on earth to be even... We were only granted one few thing—Chance, Choice and Opportunity and sometimes even these aren't recognized or granted. So, look around you, the people and animals alike have survival in common— But for man alone his conscience is his alone, but the world around him guarantees:

NO MAN IS TOTALLY FREE!!!!!!

Reality Torn—

My reality is always having less and doing more
My reality is loving but not getting close enough
I ponder the life of a man and wife and their little child
I have been so close to many things and lost all
I am blessed to stand on my own and fall the same
I see all that is to come but it is not enough Right Now
My reality is knowing more than I can ever explain
I am so happy and yet sadness is waiting for me

I know what love is and yet can't really be a part of it
I give so much of myself and I am left with only a shell
My reality is knowing right from wrong and disobeying anyway
My life is a continual struggle against my plan and that of the
Lord's
He has granted me great strength and personality and yet my heart
is not settled
My mind is constant in its plan for freedom and choice and yet my
actions and words move slower than that of my brain and heart
How can you tell someone you love them and not be there when
they need?
You?
How can you adore something so much and yet not grab hold of it?
I must tell you—I have experienced many things and witnessed
even morebut the heart of humans and that especially of a woman
I can not to this day understand
Damn, I say why is life joy and misery one in the same
Why do I have little when others have a lot?
Why do I have more than those that have not?
I ask God to save me from my own worst enemy—My Heart
I ask for guidance and understanding and nothing I hear
Maybe it is not what I want to hear and I carry on the same
For that is my mistake, I am not listening to what is said
Maybe I am looking to find answers and insight where there is
none
I dream of nothing and feel the same—I am tired now, frustrated and
disappointed
My own child is lost to me and that is disheartening, my soul is
that of an Angel but my actions are not
My compassion for humanity is more than I care to take, but that
is my gift to the world?
By no means am I a selfish person, but I need to be to find myself

Learning about Me, Yourself, and I—a lifetime goal that may never be understood

For those few who have stood in relationships when they were sad I am sorry for your suffering

For those that were happy and lost their way I am sad

For those few that have found love in abundance and are happy I am overjoyed

For those like myself trying to find peace and love that is blinding don't give up

I once knew the face of a smiling child once and there I was—ME just a guy who loved without ceasing

And today I am far removed from the she and we

Sometimes I want to just lie down and cry but no tears come

I have been stripped of all humanity, I have been dragged through the mud and back again

I have been lifted up; I have been set on high but only for a little while

I am full of disgust in our world and its leaders but whom can we blame we put them there

The human spirit is not strong enough for Unity

I am a non-confrontational man who wants to adore life and its many pleasures

And instead I get moments of serenity and joy

My love I can't explain, nor can I explain who I am, but if you need me you will find me warm and compassionate when I am not within myself

My voice is strong and my words are few, my tone is soft and yet... hard to understand

Grow I will, Succeed I might, fail again—I may but I will get up—he won't let me stay

I am tired now running from what I am, but where am I running to—I don't know

But today is my time and I will use it wisely, no more regrets and
I am not scared to say NO—my path will be revealed
I don't know where I am going or how I will get there, I can't even
say I will have company—this journey may be mine alone—
That I don't understand but if needed I will go. On my path to
Nowhere—or Eternity
All that I give comes freely from inside me
My love is true and my heart is a mess but my smile keeps shining
No more fights or arguments for me—Life is troubling enough
So, hello world it is just I trying to fit in and find a spot—I still
breathe through God's hands and Christ's salvation—strike me
down again and again
And I will still have a smile for you
This is just some of my reality

The Change of Season (Spring)

*Today I hear the sounds of the birds as the sun warmest increases and
rises earlier than it had when it was cold. The winter is close to an end
and its dry cold is nearly but a whisper now. No more clouds filled with
snow, bitter cold rain, whose destruction has caused flooding and avalanches
this season. As the branches bring fresh green leaves and flowers start their
colorful blossom. —May I too enjoy the joy of change in self and scenery
of the new days to come? Like the pollen taking wind in spring, may my
life also see new flights of fancy? For all the animals who have rested in
the dark cold winter have now sprung awake and scurry about—I too look
forward to this, the season of joyous wonder and excitement that raises
the Spirits every year at this time—for there is no season that awakes so
glorious—remember too Christ was lifted during this season. May that
be a guide to the renewed freshness and vows of life—As the chatter of
friends and neighbors flow through the air and their laughter enjoyed in
the smoke of celebration—May I too seal my livelihood with those I love
and cherish—for let this embodiment of restlessness and despair pass and*

let it be reborn and re-energized with Hope and Happiness that brings forth...Spring!

An Old Man's Thought about Summer

My God it is finally here! *Summer*!! For miles, the sky is blue, except for that tiny spot to the west. My eyes dare not look up for the glare. It's too bright—That light. Gold and white in every way.

I can see the morning dew steaming off the ground, by Joe "it's high-noon", and the concrete is smok'in, people are squinting their eyes, and laughing. Tom, our weatherman, says, "Today's high will be 90 degrees". Good Lord son, that boy can read a weather map, in the dark, with air. But by golly, he ain't out here where the humidity is 110%. Man alive, pheew! "The water hole down the way sure looks good." But I still got five hours of work to do. Well at least the chil'un (children) for you city folk, are hav'in fun.

The Lord knows in time they too will be grown and sensing an urgency to slow down time. Ev'er man and woman has their breaking point dealing with day to day life. I guess that's why people not from here keep coming to the hills or down there by the coast. Yeah, after eight or nine months of working they need a break! It is hot as "all get out." Mama ain't here no mo'. But I swear I feel her smiling up there saying, "Bring that charcoal", "I'm gett'in hungry." Yes Ma'am, I reply.

It's so hot, we are sweating but let me tell ya, I'll take this beautiful summer day any time.

Today I Felt at Home! (Fall)

Today has finally arrived the warm feeling of fall
I have been somewhat hesitant to share these feelings

but today I can no longer keep them to myself. Yes, I am happy and life is abundant

I have had some minor setbacks but nothing that I cannot overcome. I have people who love me and I love them back. People who enjoy me and what I can bring to their life.

I like seeing the leaves fall and the wind howl and the glimpse of sunshine over the rooftop. The other day I drove through Cherokee Forest and I was taken back by the scenery and all its glory—man could not have had a hand in this—it is not by chance the waters held at bay or the fallen trees thereupon them. I did see debris which man did do but why I ask—No respect, No respect for nature or his surroundings. I so felt at peace on that drive that one through the winding roads. It was a perfect day for a hike, a paddle down the river, a walk on the path, and for me the drive home. It was nice, beautiful and joyful. Yes, I was at home again, even though I grew up by the sea, I felt at home.

Knights and Wizards

The strongest and best bred Horses to ride, Shinning Armor, Swords decorated, Flags with codes of arms. Men who had the strength to wear such protection, Castles to house from the bitter cold and protect their honored.

Those Heroes and Guardians who fought bravely when needed....— Those were Knights.

The mysterious seemingly all-knowing wearing dark clothing, hidden away within the shadows—giving advice when needed, standing in the cellar working their craft—With their seeing eye that sits upon the wall or table—speak the words—move the mist—be granted a wish—to know what is to come and what has passed elsewhere...

Smell the emptiness, feel the stillness, see the mystic and know then who offer remedies, poisons, potions, and wisdom beyond belief.

They are figures or mist forever changing to suit their mood of travel, gaining an edge deceiving the eye, the eyes they do—They are about secrets and mind(will)power.... Those were the Wizards.

Together Knight and Wizards are a standing reality that helped the strongest Castles

Then and Now

As a tree has rings to show its growth and age. We as mortals are the same.

We grow quickly with all our matter but without efficient water, our minds without knowledge are nothing but withering crumpled stumps.

When you look upon a willow tree it reminds you of a bunch of obstruction and chaos. But

what are we without correct influence at a young age?

The trees that bear fruits of fig, apple, and oranges. Not forgetting bananas, pineapples and pears. We as civilized or at least we think should put such effort in each other, more people benefit from our nourishing than just the work place.

THEN

Before, fields of pine and spruce were more abundant just as the Rain Forest and Jungles of Indonesia. So, too were people's concern for others. But with industrialization, bulldozers and

Gas saws to plunder the earth of its natural riches. And we do the same with people as we pick out certain categories or types to expand their talents for use while we ignore and relocate or destroy others so as not to remind us that they need care.

As humans, right organizations look to protect wildlife and its habitats we as people especially the young. Every country has sanctuaries of historical value; every country pulls resources to invest in other cultures but how realistic is it to travel thousands of miles to save distant foliage or invest in ventures to uncover riches or artifacts. When you have a symbol NIMBY or a blind eye to those in your own community. There's a lesson to be learned from Neutral European and Poor South American countries and others. Distribute what is harvested with all—And Reinvested—

<u>*Now*</u>

Sure, and Certain

Sure, is one that knows their direction
Certain are they when they plan
Sure, is the person when they study the problem
Certain is the person when they know the subject
Sure, is one that knows self and their actions
Certain is one that tells the truth to others and self
Though things go up and must come down
One must be sure of themselves on all that they do, and
if they
are not
Certain—then I hope they are surely certain of what they are going to
    do and why…
    For these words and hints are
    SURE, and CERTAIN

The Maze

Dedicated to those who have had to use God's or Darwin's intuition of "survival of the fittest." Why God's or Darwin's theory?

Darwin suggested man had to do whatever necessary to survive in the food chain of life.

God gave us a mind, "will" to choose right and wrong either way this place "earth" is a perfect world with imperfect people

—where everyone is not equal. And at times you either will or have sinned, to—try and balance your "will" to "earth" rules. But remember Christ in all you do and thank God for your being. (In the world you will have tribulation—John16:33) Life is not hard for a Christian—it is impossible— Only Christ has lived perfectly and he died for our sins (Without me you can do nothing—John15:5) Here's to finding our way home. (He "went before them" and showed the way by the pillars of clouds and fire—Exodus13:21)

May we all find our way to both salvation and personal pursuit? It's funny how people judge, when they've only looked and lived in the tube. Read your history books, travel, read other peoples' stories and learn the lessons of the Bible. Crisis, Wars, Love, Peace all have been since creation. Some may never live or have the experience to see severe hardships but for those that do and have. It's all in the Plan—May I be given the inspiration, sight and touch to write what I feel accurately, and only a piece of what I've had to experience and see in my time to date. But what comes of my creativity comes from both my own and the world's "Eye". In both "real" and "flashback."

THE CALLING

Commissioned as an Officer in Bringing Light to the World

The Craftsman

The Crown Chakra is Open: You are in the know!!!
***Your Guides, Angels, Masters, and Teachers
are Ready to Work on your Behalf***

My Awakening

A dream about Bees gave me a new sense of clarity and reinforcement to a belief system I had been developing over the past couple of years. If you have ever questioned your existence and have a passion for doing something you never thought possible, did you ever ask yourself how you know something without learning it? Are there others taking the same journey trying to understand their part in the Universe? I chance to say you have said "Yes!"

to both questions. That's good, very good indeed. It means you have been called and you either felt, heard, or dreamt that your life would no longer be the same. My awakening was from a dream, and I thought it was important that I shared the events with you. By doing this it allowed me to look at life from a different vantage point. I am not talking street level, but something elevated like watching from above. This view is more like "Third Eye Vision."

After the Dream of Bees

I have lived and traveled to places that are both spectacular and isolated. Nothing can astound you more than being an American living abroad. The advantages the average American has are not appreciated until you have been to places that are restricted, poor and, in some cases, dangerous. Whether you are from the coast, the mountains, the suburbs, the city, or in between, dreams of being something more than you are right now can't be appreciated until you have been given the opportunities for, or are blessed with, the gift of awareness. My friend, the Dream of Bees did just that. It woke me up to the opportunity to share knowledge about exceptions, and a lesson in humility and the promise of the Universal Creator's gift of love and inspiration: manifesting all the things you desire by simple thoughts and practicing simple meditation and having faith in the energy that surrounds you.

Take a moment. You have a clear message while sleeping. You see yourself from viewpoints you never have before and suddenly you realize you're talking to a bee. Yes, a bee. Not only are you talking to the bee but it is talking to you, too. There is no anxiety, just acknowledgement that something spectacular is happening and its meaning is unfolding. Amazing how our Creator, God, or Higher Power will invite you to serve a higher purpose. When you think about all the things you want to accomplish they pale in comparison to being summoned by the Universe to join the elite team of "Light workers."

"From the standpoint of daily life, however, there is one thing we do know: that we are here for the sake of each other—above all for those upon whose smile and well-being our own happiness depends, and for the countless unknown souls with whose fate we are connected by a bond of sympathy. Many times a day I realize how much my own outer and inner life is built upon the labors of my fellow men, both living and dead, and how earnestly I must exert myself in order to give in return as much as I have received."

— Albert Einstein

Everything in the universe has a purpose. Indeed, the invisible intelligence that flows through everything in a purposeful fashion is also flowing through you.

— Wayne Dyer

But you have chosen the decision that you will no longer be blind, or accept blindly an idea, any false truth, or give energy to those things that no longer serve the greater good.

FUTURE TEMPLATE TO MOVING FORWARD

Navigating the Shift

Now that you have read my journey I would like to invite you to look at a few steps to improving your outlook and opening your mind to new ideas. I will give you a few notes under each step but the expansion of these ideas will be found in the resources section at the back of the book. In my next edition I will solely focus on these steps in more detail.

Step 1: Boundaries (no more)

For many years, settlers and villagers remained local to areas of agricultural value. They planted roots along specific areas that would support their need to survive. Along the way, someone had the foresight to move beyond the local boundaries in search of something better. Hence, the development of outposts, kingdoms, and other developed spaces. How did we move from a physical location not only in body but also in mind? The dream bees are a good example of this. The dream follows a larger than life character, The Younger YOU, from a small farming community at a coastal town. As a simple farmer, YOU and your fellow tribesman follow an Earl's direction to do "raids"—actions by early Norwegians (Vikings)/Pirates, who during certain parts of the year would go out and pilfer or pirate nearby lands.

My interpretation of local, regional, and global thinking will not be fully focused on the locality of a residence but more so on the boundaries of the individual and their mindset. Like the dream, "Bees," various characters (in your life) tend to show their disposition for what they believe in and what comforts they possess. Your bees will represent any set of characters in your life that reflect the theory I have been studying over the last five years. I have been doing my own non-contact observations on people as they interact with others. I have been taking blind notes to how they currently live and explain their beliefs as well as taken note as to on how they grew out of a stage or stayed in it if at all (their beliefs). As you shift your mindset going forward you can change your bees, and soon you will develop and begin to solidify your own ideas about your personal growth or acceptance about who you are and the life you enjoy now.

While you were reading the story of the bees and recounted several events of my own journey your inner voice to self-discovery was being charged to action. YOU are now my new friend on this journey and your new circle of friends will soon be a part of your new outlook and our new-found beliefs to maintain or change the way the Universe is providing for us all. WE will also shift into what the Universal Creator has made us to be (if we choose to accept our role).

We all know several types of "bee" personalities. How about the first type of bee (person) who is resistant to change in his religion, viewpoints, or family values? That person that won't stray too far from their norms. The question we ask or consider about ourselves or those like us who are the first type of "bee" is our personal beliefs or moral standards that hold us complacent or fearful of change. What questions would one have of such a person? The first few questions might be as follows:

Why do you stay where you are?

What do you do here?

Why do you not leave?

Those were easy, right? What might you say? What has kept you not only living in the same place for many years with little travel—maybe in a certain state of mind? You know that voice you keep hearing that might sound like you (or in my case they switch between Yoda, Rafiki, and Jiminy Cricket, and every now and then the big-headed mouse the Brain will show up).

The first questions are standard to most curious people: What about those strangers is truly inspired to hear more about you? What do you think they might ask? Yoda might say, for example, "Certain you are, Are you?"

When you look around you what do you see?

Remember that empty white room? The place your initial bees brought in the first wave of pollen? That spark. Was anyone in there with you? In my dream, it was that bee (in the voice of Yoda). Like I said in the dream, he was not threatening or unfriendly but he made me notice he was there.

What makes you take notice of your surroundings, or yourself?

I have found that in some moments I take more stock in the fact that suddenly things have gotten quiet around me. It's as if I am walking around a mall aimlessly with the mall auto-tune music on mute. Or perhaps I have just ignored all distracting noises around me because I have suddenly found myself asking, "What did I come in here for in the first place?" I also find that on a nature walk I will suddenly look out far in front of me and find an unusual cloud formation or natural stone formation and think, "Huh, that looks like…" Use your imagination here. Did you see something normal in your everyday life, or did you actually see something new?

Some of my best memories of waking to something around me or near me are the thoughts of how the sun or moon might look in certain lights. Or that feeling I am smiling for no reason. In some cases, it is my legs feeling heavy. Why am I suddenly feeling like a set of cement boots were just put on my feet? Did I eat today? Did I work out too hard the previous day?

Are there unresolved issues I need to look at?

What anxieties do I have?

What are the comforts of this local town, thought, or life that has me feeling perfectly happy to stay where I am?

Don't get me wrong, not everyone is meant to leave the hive, nest, or farm. Many of us find great joy and prosperity in staying in one place and living that life, as defined by whatever metrics (factors) or schemas (beliefs) we find fit to live by.

So we begin the journey of your soul as a Harvester of Light, whether you are a small, medium, or large beacon. Without the bee's pollen (influence-spark) we would not know the calling. As we reference bees in the story and the pollen (spark (honey)) we find that in the Bible there are several references to bees' honey—a source. We can use examples like the Beatitudes (Matthew5:1-12), (Proverbs 24:14), (Exodus 3:8), and the Dalai Lama, "...bees possess an instinctive sense of social responsibility..."

Our society, our spirit, and to some degree our energy source is declining because of a lack of nourishment. There are plenty of reports about the dying bee population which continue to affect our natural food supply. Sure, I know many of you think the labs have it covered, but how much processing has to occur before it is no longer beneficial?

We look to self care for that answer. How long before you accept your talent, your passion, your gifts before you no longer produce well or make a difference? Does it even matter to you?

What is in the mind of a homeless person, the welfare recipient, or entrepreneur that quit because of one failure—or many? Some of our most influential people failed a few times.

Most of us have some knowledge of history and how America was made. What about the historical lessons learned from Europe, Africa, Asia, and more? One time in history all the land mass was one. Then the tectonic plates split—and the boundaries that once bound us were gone.

Step 2: Local

The system of beliefs that allow you contentment and keep you from taking any unnecessary risks to your way of life allows you to only be surrounded by likeminded people who say, "You understand why I don't."

This system of thinking tends to leave you paralyzed, anxious, defensive, and sometimes even hostile when confronted with having to do something new, challenging, or improved. Have you ever met someone and they just didn't fit in your "world view"? Of course you have. We see it every day. Someone asks us about how we feel or think about some news clip, article, or some random Facebook or YouTube message or video. How do those same questions affect you coming from people close to you like friends or family? Are they like you? Do they perceive as you do? Or do you naturally find yourself avoiding certain topics because you can feel your heart beating out of your chest, or you find that you have put fingernail marks on the inside of your hand because you have clenched your fist so tight? Did you get a headache yet? Not until someone makes that comment, "How can you not see it…?" Oh those are fighting words! RIGHT! "I do not think like you," you say.

Then it snowballs. The argument is that your natural way of seeing things is fine because you live that way, nurtured to be who you are, a local person. Proud to get the town newspaper, watch the local weather channel, and live your high school dreams for life—in thought that is. What does happen when some of your classmates bypass or graduate from the local community college and go off to the university? Do they come back with these big ideas, as if they know everything? Did you have that local boy or girl go off and join the military and suddenly come back with anxiety that they could not breathe because someone told them how to do so? You found that everyone who tried out new thinking and returned home had a "hometown" aversion to "new" or expansion.

What does that even mean? It means that…let's name this bee "Stuey" from Family Guy as your guide. He's that bee that looks at change like a bad crop. Corn grows if you have three things: wind pollination, good fertile soil, and full sunshine. Pretty simple, right? Imagine the great and simple truth of simple thinking. Not that this is a bad thing by any means. Who wouldn't want to live and work around people who are just as "risk averse" or feel that the love and admiration they have gained from their peers is equally satisfying as a bee leaving the hive collecting pollen from a nearby flower? Pollination of the "local" mind is relative to the process Stuey has when all the conditions are normal and there are no threats to the pollination process.

Step 3: Regional

The system of beliefs that are followed we tend to have faith in allowing for a certain amount of acceptable risks or alliances that can be made for self-benefit. Moreover, it allows you to feel above those that associate with Stuey. Now you meet a bee called "Lexie." She is a risk taker. She can be found frolicking around the meadows or talking to all the strangers for miles. But wait a minute. One day she finds a landmark that is overgrown off to the side. The sign says here is the border of Pine, Ash, and Oak; from here in these three directions you will find Challenges, Opportunities, and Success.

Well, Lexie is excited. She quickly runs home and packs a bag. She eventually travels to each of these spots and learns things she would never have known if she had not explored. However, there is something interesting. She is comfortable knowing that there is control in her spirit by way of knowing others who like her wait for her return because she won't go too far and the information she will bring back is not too scary. They like her Tales of Pine, Ash, and Oak. She never questions what is beyond that because each time she goes to any of the places she learns a little more but not too much.

Here we are taking chances learning and exploring but for some reason complacency has struck again. Fantastic challenges, opportunities, and successes in discovery are available but the risk is just right. Our system of beliefs is still intact and those new ideas are favorable and it feels good.

Are you a Lexie? Are you comfortable picking up a newspaper, reading a new book, or going to the fair? When a stranger comes up to you, do you welcome the exchange?

How are you when someone isn't from a place within a certain distance of you? Again, this is not about location but the ability to form new ideas and change your views and actions based on new information.

Location = emotional intelligence, which turns into value added growth of your inner emotional, mental, physiological/psychological self, the emerging you = use of both the left and right brain.

Wait a second! I hear Rafiki calling, "Hello young traveler. Do you know the way?" You look around and are like, "What?" Then suddenly he repeats the question, this time with a little giggle.

You reply, "Nope, but I am good because I understand." And so you do. You found out that understanding is good, especially when there is minimal risk to your way of life. From time to time you are fine with tuning into new information but only so much.

There is peace in your mind, your spirit, and your heart. You help people around you and you find joy in that, small leaps and ease of transferring information with those you share with.

Welcome, you have arrived as the regional Harvester of Light!!!

Step 4: Global

Next is the system of beliefs or pull toward something you can't see but you know it to be true, and you know that the high risks are well worth the possible rewards that are yet to come.

The Ultimate Harvester of Light and cultivating of minds, spirits, and Energy is within ourselves and others. It is an elite calling far from anything we can explain. We just know when it comes you have to leave, and in doing so what you learn from others out there is nothing short of amazement.

For every culture you visited, for every language you attempted, and for every moment you truly sat back and meditated and truly asked for insight, synchronicity happened! Suddenly you are walking effortlessly into the shift; the THIRD EYE Chakra is beginning to tune into the life force from nature.

You start to see signs, desire to learn even more; suddenly people are coming into your life that teach you. Now you are a student and happy. You want to eat, drink, and sleep the world of Metaphysical and Spiritual truths of the Universal Creator's Laws of Abundance and Wisdom.

From here the horizons are no longer; the world is seen in vibrations of energy and light. Now you speak differently, and seek out those that can teach and be taught by you. You start to look for the Universal Teachers, Masters, Angels, and Guides, repelling the Waywards and Fallen who drain or attach to you, sucking your life force from you. You now have a new vocabulary. You seek events, you demand the blessings set aside for you. You look for a new circle of friends that inspire you, mentor you, and bring you to higher and higher realms of consciousness.

Welcome to the land of Jiminy Cricket. You become the voice of others as you are looking for the voices that call for you to live in your talents, rise to your calling, and excel in your SERVICE to OTHERS.

Step 5: Beyond boundaries

Let's take an escalated look at what happens when you move from local, regional, and global thinking, and make the personal shift towards self, the Universe, and beyond.

There is no looking back. The shift has happened. Your Chakras are aligned and you continue to seek out opportunities for Abundance, Wisdom, and Enlightenment.

Here you are assisting others in channeling, awakening, and focusing in on the POSITIVES!

You are no longer a child, teen, or adult carrying the burdens, manipulations, or fears of your genetics and ancestry. You are free in the world and are in a sense a MONK-like figure. You are now forging new paths. Things come easier to you and you are calm; you are now a person of interest. You are sought out and you welcome the opportunity to share in the Universal Energy and are providing the lessons The Creator has given you to help and inspire others.

Step 6: Check your status

This is a short survey on whether you are ready for the shift and what to do next if you are. Please see the resource section below for continued growth.

Step 7: Choices

Here you are expanding the idea that accepting the highest change brings you closer to the Universal Creator's path for you. And you benefit from continued development to accept more "light" sources, manifesting, and other metaphysical beliefs as you seek "the best knowledge practices from all sources!"

No one has been born without a heartbeat, and no one has succeeded in everything the first time. If you have ever questioned your existence and have a passion for doing something you never thought possible, this book will help you better understand and guide you into trusting your intuition and creating the right circle of support to aid you in your changes.

CHECK YOUR STATUS

Self-Evaluating Current Awareness of your Part in the Universe

1. Are you open to new information?
2. Have you been restless?
3. Who are the new people in your life?
4. Are you feeling a pull to serve others?
5. Are you aware you have less patience for those that have subjective opinions rather than objective opinions?
6. Are you aware you just don't accept things at blind or face value as you once did?
7. Can you sense entities lightly touching you, can you hear them? I feel shivers when my guides or angels are near.
8. To which of the intuitive abilities do you relate?
   i. Clairvoyance — clear seeing.
   ii. Clairsentience — clear feeling.

iii. Clairaudience — clear hearing.

iv. Claircognizance — clear knowing.

9. Have you defined your Spiritual gifts with your Talents?

10. Do you now understand the meaning of "I intend this or something better for the highest good of all involved!"

JOURNAL ENTRY

Just when I think I have learned the way to
live, life changes. —Hugh Prather

Write your Answers here:

ABOUT THE AUTHOR

In the book, "NOMADIC JOURNEY: TO SPIRITUAL AWARENESS; SEEKING WISDOM AND DISCOVERING GOD'S PLAN, IN ACKNOWLEDGING OUR GIFTS AND TALENTS," Author L.C. Smith shares his beliefs and observations on how people are internally programmed to follow a system of societal rituals and norms leaving them pondering their true purpose. Lee shares his personal dream about Bees he had while serving the U.S. military on his third Middle Eastern deployment as a sign to awaken one's self and become more aware of the self, the universe, and the "light" that is in all of us. Bees are the caretakers of the planet. Without bees, life would be a lot harder. To share the wisdom Lee uses the messages from the bees as an intuitional compass. With nearly twenty years of military leadership, over a decade of both government and business consulting experience, and currently a Clinical Psychology PsyD Candidate, Lee shares his observations and theories about people being stuck or limited in their views. We all could better use our intuition and practice meditation, surrounding ourselves with co-creators who believe that to make monumental changes in the world we must open our minds to what the universe can provide if we only ask for it.

ADDITIONAL RESOURCES

These are a few books that have helped expand my views to how I see the World.

Assassin's Creed Book Series
By Oliver Bowden

The Monk Who Sold his Ferrari
By Robin Sharma

The Secret Letters of The Monk Who Sold His Ferrari
By Robin Sharma

The Legend of the Monk and the Merchant: Twelve Keys to Successful Living
By Terry Felber (Author), Dave Ramsey (Foreword, Contributor)

Accidental Saints: Finding God in all the wrong people
By Nadia-Bolz-Weber

Excuse Me Your Life is Waiting: The astonishing power of feelings
By Lynn Grabhorn

The Moses Code: The most powerful manifestation tool in the History of the World
By James Twyman

Johnathan Livingston Seagull
By Richard Bach

Mentor: The Kid & The CEO
By Tom Pace with Walter Jenkins

Printed in the United States
By Bookmasters